About the author

Since finishing as a finalist in *Love Island* Series 8 in 2022, Tasha Ghouri has established herself as a prominent figure in the fashion industry, collaborating with sustainable and high-end brands. In addition to her fashion endeavours, Tasha remains deeply committed to supporting causes close to her heart.

Tasha is the first ever Pre-Loved Ambassador for eBay and serves as a brand ambassador for several premium brands, including L'Oréal Paris and Hot Diamonds. In 2024, she was also a finalist on BBC's *Strictly Come Dancing*.

A passionate advocate for inclusivity, Tasha uses her platform to encourage individuals to embrace their disabilities, which she refers to as 'superpowers'. She hosts her own podcast, *Superpowers with Tasha*, where she engages in conversations with prominent guests about their unique strengths and experiences. Through her work, she aims to challenge societal taboos and raise awareness of issues related to disability and inclusivity.

Tasha is also a proud Global Ambassador for DeafKidz International and actively supports charities such as RNID and NDCS.

your
super
power

Embrace what
makes you different

TASHA GHOURI

PIATKUS

PIATKUS

First published in Great Britain in 2025 by Piatkus

1 3 5 7 9 10 8 6 4 2

A CIP catalogue record for this book
is available from the British Library.

ISBN 978-0-349-44116-0

Typeset in Dante by M Rules
Printed and bound in Great Britain by
Clays Ltd, Elcograf S.p.A.

Papers used by Piatkus are from well-managed forests
and other responsible sources.

Piatkus
An imprint of
Little, Brown Book Group
Carmelite House
50 Victoria Embankment
London EC4Y 0DZ

The authorised representative
in the EEA is
Hachette Ireland
8 Castlecourt Centre
Dublin 15, D15 XTP3, Ireland
(email: info@hbgi.ie)

An Hachette UK Company
www.hachette.co.uk

www.littlebrown.co.uk

I dedicate this book to everyone out there who is a superhero in their own way. Always remember, no one else is you and that's your biggest power.

contents

My love letter to you ...   ix

Introduction   1

Chapter One   Love   23

Chapter Two   Respect   53

Chapter Three   Growth   81

Chapter Four   Resilience   103

Chapter Five   Change   125

Chapter Six   Determination   149

Chapter Seven   Learning   169

Chapter Eight   Responsibility   179

                 My new superpower   195

                 Epilogue   203

                 Acknowledgements   207

my love letter to you . . .

Hello – and thank you to you for picking up this book!

First things first: welcome to my life, my journey, my life lessons and my mistakes. I've gone through many obstacles, as we all have (life is hard!); some you may know about, others I'll share with you over these pages. Somehow, with time, I've overcome them; if not completely, I've learned how to handle my response to them. And yes, I know there are still many more ahead of me, but I'm sure that some of the skills I've picked up in the past twenty-five years will help me navigate the ups and downs we all face going forward. Fingers crossed.

Now, let me put my belief about life's hurdles front and centre at the outset: just getting up and getting on with it can be very, very tough for all of us at various points, but if we can stay strong, humble and determined to push through the hard times, I think we'll be OK. It's the hard times that make us grow and help us achieve amazing things. You can probably think of a few examples immediately, can't you? You will get knockbacks – we all do – but it's about how you stand up and brush yourself off afterwards. It's about how you rebalance and find your feet in a positive way that really sums up who you are and how far you can go. The fact you've been drawn to pick up this book tells me already that you are destined for greatness; a world full of much more than others may think you are capable of and assign to you. You are here for a reason: believe in that and in yourself. I believe in you.

'Life's a climb, but the views are great.' That's my motto, and I'll be reminding you of it as we make our way through the following eight chapters. Never give up, no matter how hard the climb gets – because it's worth it. Trust me. Once you see that view, take it in, enjoy it and celebrate your successes, big or small. Always be your own cheerleader; it's not selfish or vain to be proud of yourself.

Surround yourself with good, positive people who uplift you and want what's best for you. It's OK to cut negative people out of your life – sometimes having that energy around you is draining. So put yourself first (some might even say selfishly), as your own happiness is your first priority. Trust me, once you cut out that negativity, you'll feel a whole new energy shift and be able to focus more on the good around you.

I hope you enjoy reading this book and take something from it. And I look forward to going on this journey together, *learning many new life lessons, from page to page, day to day. Let's do this!*

Lots of love,
Tasha xx

introduction

It's a strong word: superpower. When I think of the word superpower it makes me think of super heroes wearing capes, leaping off buildings to save the world. I don't swing from skyscrapers or eject ice from my fingertips, so who am I to write a book about finding your superpower? Why do I think I can help you harness that which makes you different and turn it into something pretty spectacular? Well, although my version of finding ways to be strong and bold is less Marvel and more mindful, it's still a world of superpowers, I assure you. Let's start with my story.

My first big life-plot twist is that I was born completely deaf, in a small town called Thirsk in North Yorkshire, a pretty place that's more or less in the middle of nowhere and where everyone knows everyone, which can be a good or a bad thing, depending on what you're up to. Well, that's how it felt for me growing up there, anyway. My parents realised I was deaf when I was about twelve months old, which is quite late for it to be discovered, but there were no hearing tests for newborns back then, they were introduced years later. The penny finally dropped when they noticed I wasn't responding to certain sounds other babies would react to, and when they spoke to me, I wouldn't look at them. So this is how and where my journey to finding my superpower began. From the outside looking in, my future may have looked bleak – difficult, at best. But my path took a different turn . . .

My deafness was a complete shock for my whole family; there was no history of it on either side. But over the years, as much as it helped me to dig deep and find my superpowers, it did the same for all of them. They had to adjust to a new life they'd never have predicted, which was especially hard for my older brother, Alex, who suddenly had this baby sister who got most of the attention. No one prepared us for what our lives would look like, and, as I share later, it really took its toll on my parents' marriage. But as I wrote in my letter above, it's these unexpected challenges that can make you grow the most, and all four of us learned a lot, navigating this new world of disability together.

London calling

The second phase of my story begins when I left Yorkshire and moved to London, on my own, aged eighteen. I wanted to be a dancer and although I loved the small town I grew up in, I knew it was unlikely to give me the career I dreamed of. I was desperate to dance, despite my deafness, and despite the fact I was constantly told it wasn't a proper career. My passion and determination were too strong not to try.

London had it all, and I was excited to get there. I couldn't wait to start a new chapter and become the version of me I always wanted to be. I'd always been independent and brave – they are two things that I think being deaf gave me from a very early age – so a move to the big city to pursue my dream of being a dancer seemed like something I had to do, however scary or difficult. I knew I had to go where the opportunities were; they wouldn't come and find me. And with that move I grew so much as a person. I had to learn how to stand on my own two feet, meet new friends and live by myself.

It was in London that a modelling agent approached me one day, and a whole other world opened up. I'd never thought about modelling, but I had always loved fashion and decided to grab every show or shoot offered to me, even if it meant taking risks sometimes. Then someone saw my work, and that's when ITV Studios contacted me (on my Instagram DMs), again, very unexpectedly, saying, 'We're casting for a love show – do you want to chat to us about going on it?' It was pretty obvious it was *Love Island*, and I thought, being single, *OK, I can talk to them about it.*

Countless Zoom and phone calls followed – the whole audition process took about three months. Then, when one of the producers called to say I'd been cast, I freaked out. The guy on the other end of the phone was like, 'Tasha, are you still there? Can you hear me?' I said, 'Yes. Of course.' It was a potentially life-changing moment for me. Having previously had very, very bad luck in the love department, I had nothing to lose. I'd be the first deaf person on *Love Island*, and that was too big for me to turn down. It would mean I would get to represent the deaf community on a show where image was everything and that meant so much to me.

As we all know, within the TV industry there is still not enough representation of people who have disabilities, or even who are different. But I would get to spend the summer in a villa with gorgeous men *and* break down a few barriers, showing a big audience that a deaf person can be confident and chatty. It was a win–win I thought – and the bet paid off. *Love Island* has been a great launching pad for where I am now, with a podcast which focuses on the stories of inspirational people who have overcome mental and physical challenges . . . and this book! It has helped me reach out to so many people I'd never otherwise have got to hear about or learn from.

The past is history, tomorrow is a guess, today is a present

And that's how I got here today. When I look back, I think having courage has been what's driven me from the beginning, although it wasn't something that came in a day. I've had to work on it and got better at it since I moved to London and hit my twenties. I wasn't always as confident as a person, especially in high school, where I was quite introverted. I don't know if I was ashamed of my deafness back then, but I found it difficult to accept and talk about it. If people asked me about my condition or my cochlear implant (more on what this is in a bit), I'd shut them down. I'd more often than not tell them I wasn't ready to talk about it; I was still trying to work out who I was and how I wanted to share my disability, which is hard in my generation when social media demands you share and post and discuss everything. I knew I was different, and I felt an internal pressure to be an advocate for others like me, but part of me just wanted to hide.

A parent's view
My dad gives you the lowdown

I was too young to remember or understand what was going on with me at the start of my super-power journey. Luckily, my dad, Tarek, and mum, Nicky, remember it all, and will share their side of my story throughout the book – not only to fill in the bits I can't remember but to help other parents understand and care for their child who has disabilities or difficulties, and perhaps to help them feel less alone or frustrated. Tarek says:

Tasha's disability was hidden from us at first. Babies do not talk, but they do respond to facial expressions, lip movement, arm waving and even vibration through floors, so for all we knew Tasha was hearing. Red flags started to appear when she was around eleven to twelve months old and she would not turn around when spoken to from behind. There started a journey of tests and appointments, and she was diagnosed with a severe sensory hearing loss in one ear and profound sensory loss in the other at around fourteen months. A sensory hearing loss means the small hairs in the cochlear part of the inner ear were damaged or non-existent at birth. To explain: sound is heard through the ear via soundwaves and the hairs are stimulated by those waves. As the hairs move, they create an electrical impulse, which is sent to the brain which computes the sound.

Of course, initially, I was like a rabbit in headlights — stunned and dazzled by the unknown challenges that lay ahead. Naturally, there were all the usual things you would do for a child, such as a bedtime story, feeding them, playing with them, etc., but with Tasha, more time and extra activities were needed. The toys we purchased were more aligned with learning and developing speech, rather than just play. We adapted to ensuring we were facing her anytime we were communicating and not covering our mouths. We would use dolls with her and have conversations using our own faces to express what the doll could be saying. Tasha loved her Bratz dolls; she would play with them for hours. She would mimic a conversation between two dolls, one in each hand, talking for them, yet the words were totally unintelligible. It is interesting that she was thinking what they would be saying to each other, yet the words were not there.

I am a DJ and the house was always filled with music, which brought Tasha joy as she could feel the bass through my standing speakers, which stood on a wooden floor. She seemed to be set free by music, and when that was combined with a pop video on the TV, she would come alive.

During her childhood, we suffered some knockbacks, such as support at school being revoked or reduced, but we put our faith in social services, the audiologists and the doctors. We joined groups for the deaf community and could see how other deaf people got on with things: they had jobs, they managed to go shopping, they lived happy lives. We saw the possibility of technology help-ing Tasha and researched cochlear implants. As part of her assessment for an implant, we were introduced to a young girl called Josie, who had received one around eight months previously. I was taken aback by the clarity of her speech and that she could say the word 'gymnas-tics'. This may not sound like a great achievement for a ten-year-old – however, this word is full of 'soft letters' that hard-of-hearing/deaf children cannot usually repli-cate. Letters such as F, P, S are soft when spoken and do not hold a strong lip pattern either, so they are difficult letters to decipher for the lip reader. I remember that day vividly as a light-bulb moment for me.

Tasha's implant operation was a success. Cochlear implants are not a silver bullet for normal hearing, but they create a wonderful solution for people with a sensory hearing loss when used with other techniques, such as lipreading. But when Tasha was sixteen, right in the middle of her A-levels, the internal part of the implant stopped working, which meant a further operation. For this period, she could not hear, and having dropped sign language nine years previously to develop and train her brain for the implant, she was left very isolated and alone for three months. It was painful to watch. I felt knocked back, so I can only imagine how Tasha felt. It was as if we had gone full circle back to the beginning. I felt so much pain and sadness for her in this period that even typing this brings me to tears. But I dug deep and wrapped my arms, my soul and my love around her to help her through it as best I could.

Sharing is caring

As I've said, one of my biggest superpowers is having had solid, good people – like my parents and my brother – around me from day one of my journey. They have allowed me to get comfortable with who I am and encouraged me to talk about what makes me special. I can clearly recall a life-defining moment when a little bell rang inside me, telling me I was different and that I should step up and share my story;

that I had what it took inside me to make a difference. It happened when I was training to be a dancer at the Creative Academy, a university that offered a professional dance programme, after I'd left school. As part of my studies, I had to perform a dance I'd been working on for weeks in front of hundreds of teachers and students. I was halfway through when my cochlear implant fell out. Suddenly, my world fell silent. There was no beat to follow, no rhythm to guide me. Just me in my own head. My first instinct was to run away, but I knew I'd be annoyed with myself afterwards for giving up. 'Just keep going,' I said to myself, *just keep going*. And something clicked. I was still on beat; I was capable of keeping score in my head. I could do it. 'Keep going for it,' I told myself, as my body made the moves and took the steps I'd been practising so hard to perfect. As I finished the routine, my eyes fell on the choreographer, Josh, who is now my best friend, and I saw tears streaming down his proud face. *You did it. You can do anything*, he mouthed to me. And in that moment, I knew it was true. If I was brave, nothing could hold me back. And, as people applauded me, and Josh wiped away the happy tears, I felt like I'd opened my wings and could fly.

From that day, I realised I needed to stop letting my deafness define me. I had to switch up my brain to appreciate it as something that made me unique, rather than something that was holding me back. I needed to stop doubting myself, and not think that because I was deaf I couldn't do this or that. I thought, *You know what – I am going to stop hiding who I am, go for everything I want in this world and be unashamedly me, pros and cons, highs and lows.*

And this is what I hope to instil in you over the course of this book: the belief in yourself to show people (and, most importantly, yourself) that you can achieve anything, no matter how big or small. What's more, by sharing your story, you could help someone else take the first step on their own difficult journey. Sharing is a way of caring for those around you, by encouraging them to find themselves and be proud of who they are. And this brings me back to why I'm writing this book: I want to help *you* become a butterfly and find your wings.

It's not going to be easy – believe me, I know – so be prepared. Before the moment when I danced in front of a huge crowd, when I owned my shit and had faith in myself, there was anger, fear, self-doubt and lots of other nasty, niggling feelings and emotions. There were lots of slammed doors, lots of crying fits, lots of low moments where I didn't know what to do next. I've learned the hard way that you can only get past an obstacle by taking it on and getting the better of it. And each time you climb over a wall in front of you, you'll get stronger and smarter. It's true that obstacles never go away completely – they'll pop up when you least expect it and get in your way or slow you down – but you know the secret now: you have it within you to overcome the obstacles and, more than that, each obstacle is an opportunity for growth.

Leave your ego behind

Your superpower isn't just about you, and your disability or quirk isn't only a chance for *you* to grow – it's an opportunity for your loved ones, too. So remove your ego from the equation. My parents and my brother were there for me, picking me up every day, encouraging me to smash through hurdles and keep going. They've put the work in since I was one year old, and I wouldn't be me without them.

Always be grateful to those who help you embrace your strengths and push your doubts to the side. My dad said, when he was a guest on my podcast, that both he and my mum had blamed themselves for my deafness. They used to climb into bed each night and struggle with a deep, unhealthy sense of guilt that they had done something to cause it. It makes me so sad that I only found this out last year, and that they had both been suffering with these feelings in silence for so long. I was so glad when he finally confessed, and I could assure them both that I knew, and had always known, that it was just something that happened. And that it has shaped me for the better as a person. 'You've taught me to be strong and resilient,' I told them. 'You've taught me to be humble, to be grateful. You have nothing to feel guilty about.'

Can you feel the love?

When I told my family I had been selected to go on *Love Island*, they didn't know how to feel about it at first. I guess most parents might feel worried, but I assured them I wouldn't be having sex on camera, stripping off naked or doing anything else that might embarrass them or myself. I'm not that kind of girl anyway, and they knew that, but I guess they were being protective, and my dad has always worried about my career – dancer, model and now Love Islander. But my parents have always been two of my biggest supporters and they knew how much it meant to me to use it as a platform to raise awareness for the deaf community and to show that having a disability shouldn't hold anyone back. It was then that they told me to jump in with both feet. They also both knew that I was a grafter and would give everything I had to reach my goals. After all, I got my work ethic from them. They both came from nothing, from quite poor backgrounds, and worked hard to build the lives they wanted, becoming role models for me in the process. Just by watching them, with nothing said, I knew conscientiousness was key. It's funny, haven't you found that the harder you work, the luckier you get?

Finding my superpower

My dad was the first person who told me I should think of my deafness as a superpower – that sometimes, for all of us, what seems like darkness can actually fuel great strength. I knew instantly what he meant. I got my cochlear implant put in when I was five, but I could take it out whenever I wanted and be deaf again – and I do have moments when I love being deaf. I can have a peaceful, relaxing shower without anything interrupting my daydreams, I can take it out at night and have peaceful sleep and I can go for a walk and not be bothered by traffic. My dad's take on deafness allowed me to embrace my disability in a fresh way, with a new label. And we can all do that! Whatever makes you feel different, brave and strong – claim it as your superpower: your anxiety, your ADHD, your shortsightedness, your bad-skin days, or your depression . . . Whatever it is, re-label it and say it out loud. Take whatever you've thought of in negative terms (or others have pointed out to you as a negative trait) and make it your own. When I do this, I *do* feel like a Marvel character in a superhero movie. And on my down days, when I'm feeling low or just not as confident as I normally do, I remember my dad's reframing and say: 'Tasha you have a superpower. You've got this. You can do it.' And it works.

Your superpower doesn't have to be a disability; it can be a personality trait or quirk, or physical feature that has at times made you feel vulnerable or different or less than. Are you shy? Short or tall? Do you find certain social settings difficult? Your differences have the power to make you strong, empathetic, brave, witty and understanding. Never give up on yourself.

Your secret weapon

The biggest lesson my parents taught me was to be kind to everyone. Because everyone is battling something, whether you know about it or not – visible or invisible scars from disabilities, differences or trauma . . . a superpower they have yet to come to grips with, perhaps. I try to remember that every day. And it's also a good tip to be kind to people who aren't nice to you. That's right: kill them with kindness. It disarms, weakens and confuses them. And you get to sleep soundly at night. Kindness is your secret weapon, whatever stage you are at in life.

I think I first learned how important kindness was when it was very clearly missing from significant parts of my life: when I was getting bullied at school. I remember thinking of the old saying, if you can't say anything nice, don't say anything at all, and wondered why people seemed to struggle with that. Keep it to yourself, I'd think when one of my peers posted something nasty about me online. And unfortunately I was forced to revisit this feeling when I got out of Love Island and was hit with lots more spite and nastiness, this time from strangers. People who'd never met me – people who'd just seen me on screen – were ripping me apart. And with glee! But I'd put myself in the spotlight, in a position to get judged cruelly, so what was I going to do?

As others tore me down, my parents' advice on being kind really kicked in. The nasty comments said everything about the person making them – nothing about me. In fact, the minute I got out of the show, my mum and dad sat me down and gave me a brief rundown of some of the things that had been said or written about me. They wanted to prepare me for what had been said and, in that moment, we all agreed it was best that I tried to avoid looking at the hateful posts. If I'd started to look, I'd have ended up down a deep, dark and depressing hole that wouldn't have been good for me. I had some idea of the negativity people continued to throw at me, but managed to mostly avoid the shade. I was made aware that people were negatively focusing on my deaf accent, so I did take that as an opportunity to jump on TikTok and Instagram and post videos explaining that I was deaf, and how that could affect a person's voice, to try and educate and spread awareness. That would shut people down – it's more empowering than if I'd made personal comments about their looks or called them names. I'd coach people to be kinder by being kinder. And I even got a few apologies popping up in my DMs.

We never know what is happening behind closed doors. We don't know why people look, talk or behave the way they do – and that goes for the bullied and the bullies. People don't always present their real selves, especially with social media, a magnet for toxicity and jealousy. The keyboard warriors could be hurting inside and not know how to articulate that pain. So I like to do a Michelle Obama, and when they go low, I go high. This forgiveness hasn't come easily or quickly for me. I've had to really work on it, as I've worked on myself. But I've learned the hard way that when someone is mean to you, it's because they want to reduce you to their level; they want a reaction – and I won't give them one. You have to stay calm, allow them to be who they are, and be better. And if they carry on? Delete and block, delete and block, delete and block. You do not have to put up with their cruel words or actions whether in real life or online – you have the power to get rid of them (see pages 66–68).

Anyway, you can vibrate at a much higher level when you choose kindness. And this starts with self-kindness always. Choose yourself. The trolls want you to be insecure and sad, but you need to take your power back – add self-kindness to your superpower pack! So if you're going through a rough time with bullies at school, at work or on social media, re-member to stay focused on what you can control, and know they are operating from a place of insecurity. And hang in there! I remember school being such a hard time, especially between the ages of thirteen and sixteen. I can recall being miserable a lot of the time. At that age, everyone is trying to figure out who they are, while looking around them and fearing that everyone else knows what's going on and has life all figured out. But they don't. And that's another secret I want to share up front: that even if we pretend to, none of us has all the answers. Especially in our teens, we know so little – when there's exams, friendship dramas, clashes with parents around rules and boundaries . . .

When I was at school, a fellow pupil basically set up a public hate page about me, with truly awful things on there like telling me to go kill myself, all written from the safety of her keyboard, of course. I had to be very strong-minded just to get up, get dressed and go to school every day. How did I do it? My parents told me it wouldn't be for ever, and I listened to them. I looked ahead. I knew I was destined for bigger, better and kinder things. I focused on what I could control: revising for my exams, continuing with dance classes every afternoon after school (which provided me with a happy, safe place) and I cherished my supportive friends (helping them through tough days, too).

Bullying, whenever it happens, is a horrible thing to endure. Don't keep it to yourself, speak up and speak out, and seek help. You are not the one who needs to be squashed and silenced – your bully is! My parents and I went to my school's headteacher, who was great and sorted it out. I'm also not ashamed to say I went to therapy – a space where I could talk about my feelings without worrying anyone. But truly, the best piece of advice I can give you if you're having a tough time at school right now is to remember it'll soon be over and you'll never have to see any of those people ever again. I haven't seen any of my classmates – or my bully – since I left. So have faith – things will get better – and be patient. I promise you'll get through it.

The book of you

Over the next eight chapters, I want you to feel understood and motivated to manifest your strongest, most powerful self, however that looks for you. There is still not enough representation in books, films and on television for all of us to feel included and supported, but I hope this book will help us get one step closer. I don't want anyone to feel how I felt growing up, when there was no one I could relate to in the public eye, the deaf community being hidden from view in the media. I'm writing this book to encourage you to know, whatever your disability, that the extra work you've had to do just to get in the mix of everyday life is going to make you fierce.

It's hard enough figuring out who you are without the extra weight of a disability on top of everything. But I'm here to tell you it doesn't define you – it's just a part of you. And it's a part that can make you stronger, kinder and original.

Across the coming chapters, I'll share my advice and tips on boosting confidence, and I'll be bringing in people I admire to give you little pep talks, too. And, as I said, my parents will have a few words to share as well because so much of our own ability to embrace our power comes from the people around us who nurture it, occasionally at their own expense. (Top-secret fact: it can be hard to live with a superhero – so cherish those who stick around!)

You can do anything you set your mind to. Each amazing person I meet reminds me of that. When I hear a superpower story I think, *If they can do it, so can I*! When I interview people for my podcast, I get a good reality check, too. Some of these people have been through so much – worse stuff than I have – but they still show up in the world with smiles on their faces and a few wise words to impart. They've got up, got out and done what they needed to do. Legends. And after each chat, I've learned a new skill that I've wanted to implement in my own life. I hope this book will give you that kind of boost. Then you can go on and motivate others, taking some of those tips with you. Every story shared has a domino effect, knocking another person into action, then another, pushing them forward. Growing up, I found it hard to talk about my disability, but then, when I saw the positive feedback I'd get from a post, or when I gave a talk at a school, I realised that instead of being embarrassed if I shared, I'd help people. And I learned that most people have their own self-doubts, which you can help disperse for them. I'm human, so I still have bad days, but I know now that everyone is fighting a battle – often one you don't know about.

Move on up

You can climb that wall. You can climb that mountain. And at the top, you can stop and enjoy the view – before you move on and find the next one to scale. Life is a series of climbs. They never stop. But they are worth it. Remember this:

- Every summit reached will be another opportunity for you to feel proud of yourself and give love to those who gave you a leg up along the way, and to share your advice on how you got there.

- Don't bottle anything up – you'll explode. Make notes in this book as you work your way through it: ideas and solutions for you to keep on the ascent towards the life you want to lead. Stay focused on your goals, and don't compare yourself to others. That's a losing game that will slow you down and distract you from reaching the pinnacle of your mountain.

- Other people will do great things – use that as a motivator, not a deflater or detractor. You are ascending a different hill. You are on your own journey, and not in competition with anyone but the best version of yourself.

- It's down to you, ultimately. You have to reach new heights alone. No one else can do it for you. Your family, friends and mentors may be able to offer you occasional support and a helping hand when you need it, and even when you don't need it, you know they will always be there. But this is for you and when you stare up to the top of that mountain, take a deep breath and look inwards. It is what *you* are made of that will take you to the summit.

I hope that you will love this book as much as I do. It's for you if you're feeling alone or misunderstood, if you're confused about what you can do next, if you're struggling with being different, if you're riddled with self-doubt. And it's for you if you're a teenager, a twentysomething or a parent who is trying to get their life on track. This book is for everyone who hasn't had it easy or just needs a little bit of encouragement to be the version of you that you have always wanted to be. It is for those people, regardless of their age or background or health status, who need a cheerleader to guide them to a place where they feel happier, safer and more powerful. For the next eight chapters, I'm honoured that your cheerleader will be me.

Not all superheroes wear capes. Some travel in wheelchairs, wear cochlear implants or attend regular appointments with a doctor, therapist or dermatologist – or simply can't leave the house. Your superpower is nothing to be ashamed of or embarrassed about. It makes you unique. You are so amazing. You are incredible. And, like all superheroes, you have something to give, to help yourself and those you care about.

When you can embrace your most authentic self, you will flourish and enable those around you to flourish, too. Remember, life's a climb, but the views are great. So let's start climbing.

chapter one

love

If you don't love yourself, how in the hell you gonna love somebody else?

RuPaul

The first love any of us experiences is usually family love.

We'd always been a tight-knit bunch, my incredible parents, my lovely big brother and me, but undoubtedly, my deafness diagnosis and subsequent operations and treatments threw a spanner into the works and put everyone under a strain. Alex and I didn't have a great sibling relationship for much of my childhood because I think the focus on my health made him feel neglected and resentful at times, and that showed itself in anger towards my parents when he was a teenager. Then my parents got divorced when I was eight years old – another huge hurdle for our little family on top of my deafness. It wasn't the most civil, calm divorce in the world and it massively affected me and my brother. It still affects me. I think children feel the effects of their parents splitting up whatever age they are, however it happens.

When your parents get divorced

I didn't fully understand what was happening to our little family unit when my parents decided to split up. I was only eight and obviously there were a lot of 'adult' things they didn't share with me and Alex, as we were too young to understand and they wanted to protect us. It wasn't until I was a teenager that I asked my dad what had happened. Ultimately, like many marriages today, they grew apart and decided to split up. I will be honest, it wasn't nice or plain sailing – it was tough for them both, and for us as a family.

My mum and dad started their relationship when they were both so young, and while they had many happy years of marriage together, loving each other and raising Alex and me together, there were just some things they couldn't get through as a couple any more. I don't want to go into all of the gory details as it was their relationship and they have both now moved on and are happy. I certainly wouldn't disrespect them by sharing what is their story. Not all relationships work out and that is OK. It took me a long time to realise this. I was really upset when they got divorced. Of course no one wants their parents to split up, or even meet anyone new for that matter, but, actually, what my mum and dad have been through with their divorce, and then both going on to find happiness again, has taught me that sometimes you do have to go your separate ways to find what you are looking for, and most of the time you do end up so much happier.

It really did teach me so much about life and love, watching those two go through their divorce. There were so many contrasting emotions happening at the same time. It made me face the fact, early on in my life, that romantic relationships weren't going to be easy, that everyone wants and needs different things – and it doesn't work if only one of you in the partnership is fulfilled and content. I learned a lot from their separation; the biggest lesson being about forgiveness. I had to accept my parents weren't together any more and move on. I closed the chapter, which was made easier when I eventually realised they were happier apart than they had been together. They are now both with people more suited to them, which confirms my belief that everything really does happen for a reason. With hindsight, I know that shifting my thinking around their split was really the first time I used my biggest superpower tool: turning a negative into a positive.

My parents' divorce also helped to give me a more realistic view of love. Children can have an idealised Disney view of romance, marriage and happy-ever-afters, so will inevitably feel disappointed and let down – in themselves and others – when they can't achieve it. But the UK has a divorce rate of nearly 50 per cent now, so we need to accept that endings aren't always like happy fairytales. Sadly, as brave as we are

when we enter a new romance, we have to be realistic as
we leave it, and be gentle and kind to ourselves. Our hearts
will need time to recover. I learned these lessons early when
I was forced to see my parents as human beings with flaws,
not just as my mum and dad. I witnessed my parents as real
people – with their own shit and drama and hormones – who
made their way through the mess while never losing track
of being good parents to me and Alex. It was hard being the
'messenger in the middle' during the period when they wer-
en't speaking to each other, and splitting our time between
their two homes, but Alex and I always knew they loved us.

Love Island gave me an unexpected gift, in that it finally got
my parents in a room together again – yes, that's how long it
took them to actually speak to each other. Because I wasn't
there to be the middleman (I wasn't able to communicate
with the outside world while in the villa) they had to communicate directly. And because they couldn't call me to check I
was OK when they saw me crying on television, the next best
person – the only other person who loved me as much as they
did – was the other one of them. *Love Island* thawed them out.
They will now text or chat a bit, which would have been un-
thinkable before. They have stopped being enemies and this
has made my life a lot less stressful – and probably theirs, too.

A Parent's View

Tasha's dad Tarek on divorce

Tasha's mum requested a divorce when Tasha was eight and Alex was thirteen. I had been through my own parents' break-up when I was thirteen, so kind of understood the ramifications for children. We separated quite quickly and, sadly, with animosity between us. Unfortunately, this diluted – in fact, it removed – a joined-up approach to parenting. Although we shared custody equally, we ended up parenting differently and separately for many years. I cannot say for certain whether this helped or hindered Tasha's development, but I do remember her and her brother's raw emotion on the subject. I would sit with them both and talk a lot about feelings and I bought them each a diary to write their feelings down. I, too, had one – to set an example that it was OK. I would open up and share some of my feelings in an attempt to get them to do likewise and it worked.

For the stability of the kids and continuity of friendships in the immediate area for them both, I remortgaged to keep the family home. The same year the separation happened the family cat died and so did the kids' pet rabbit. My father had died also. It was not an easy time personally for me, but the kids became my one and only focus. Without a doubt this was a difficult period for them both, but in some ways it likely enabled them both to grow a thick skin and learn a lot about relationships and parenting.

Alex, Tasha's brother, deserves a medal and a mention. Naturally, he loved his little baby sister when she was born. We did our best to unite them in every way and ensure they received equal attention. Looking back, though, Tasha naturally took up more time, and with other commitments such as work, household matters and having some time to ourselves, for sure he felt neglected sometimes. He is, however, super proud of Tasha and all she is achieving.

Reflections on heartbreak

Everyone – no matter who they are or how they may be different – is deserving of love. Yet a child of divorce will carry a sense of pain and failure around love with them. I know I did when I met Andrew. My parents' divorce left me with a fear of love, and I've really found it hard to trust people and open up to friendships. I have six friends – that's literally it – and that's because I am so picky about who to trust. The weird thing is I am an extrovert who can chat to anyone, but I don't let them in, or get deep with many people. Because of what happened between my mum and dad, and seeing up close that people who once loved and trusted each other can cause so much hurt, I got scared off from deeper relationships of any sort.

Going into *Love Island*, I put myself in a vulnerable position. Looking for love, with people watching my every move in a game-show format, while being cautious, and trying to take my time talking to lots of different boys in the villa probably came across in the wrong way and was not a reflection of how I would date in the real world – no one talks to lots of boys all at once! In my head, from day one, Andrew was the only man I was truly interested in, but my fear and trust issues meant I couldn't just focus on him; I had to get to know the others as well. And, spoiler alert, there is a lot that goes on behind the scenes that is cut or not shared but the producers needed to make an entertaining show. I don't regret going on there, though, because I met Andrew, and we went on to have two and a half amazing years together. He was the first man I ever let in, which I'd never done before in a romantic relationship. In the past, I had set up barriers. But with Andrew, as soon as we started to build our connection properly and openly, towards the end of the series, I felt safe.

It took time, but I think anyone who has been through a parents' divorce will know it shapes (and harms) your ideas about love. Take care of your heart and remember:

- Give yourself time.
- Don't force anything.
- Honour that gut feeling.
- Being the child of divorce can be another part of your superpower armoury, allowing you to know as much what you *don't* want as what you do want.
- When you know, you know and you shouldn't force something as important as love.

My Top Five Films about Love

1. *Endless Love* - it's such a fun young-love story, about a girl whose dad does not like the guy she loves so much ... but eventually he accepts him.
2. *Eat Pray Love* - I love how Liz, the main character, goes on a journey of finding herself and then finds someone to love at the end.
3. *The Notebook* - a real classic. True love always finds its way, and the couple in this film find their way back to one another because they love each other.
4. *No Hard Feelings* - if you want a comedy romance, this is the one for you! I was in absolute belly laughs the whole time.
5. *The Fault In Our Stars* - this is a real weepy, but such a beautiful story of two lovers.

Communication is key

In relationships it is important to talk. It is natural to argue with your partner, you are not always going to agree on everything and there may be times when you rub each other up the wrong way. We can also find ourselves disagreeing with friends or family. No relationship is perfect, but it's how you deal with these little hurdles that is important. I never like to leave things in a bad way and go to bed after an argument. Bad vibes disrupt sleep and carry it on into another day. If you wake up and you still haven't solved an issue, you feel weighed down. No one needs that – life is hard enough.

So the best advice I can give anyone, in any relationship, really – family, romantic or friendship – is to communicate well:

- Locate the problem, and work on solving it together.
- Even in the tightest, most close-knit relationships you're still two separate individuals with your own opinions, needs, goals and wants. Don't lose yourself.
- You will disagree, you will annoy each other, there will be niggles. Nothing is one-sided. Don't expect hearts and flowers 24/7.
- Don't be afraid to compromise. Compromise isn't about changing who you are as a person – it's about finding space for both of you to be happy and fulfilled and listened to.
- It's about what works for you mutually. Keep other people and their opinions out of your relationship if need be.

Finding alone time

Even when you're in a relationship it's important to have some me time. If you are in your twenties especially, there can be so much outside pressure on paving a path for yourself, getting on a career ladder, building a home and a social network that having time to yourself is crucial to unwind, focus on your needs and get the restorative peace and quiet you deserve after a busy week of work. Me time for me could be as simple as getting into bed with a cup of tea for a Netflix marathon. Some people might think craving alone time is bad. But it's not. You won't always want to watch the TV shows your partner wants to watch, and it's OK to have different interests. Focus on yourself. Do the things you need to do to refill your cup, and then come back together replenished. It helps. And you don't even need to leave the house.

Sorry seems to be the hardest word

I used to be so stubborn as a child. I would never say sorry. I saw it as a weakness to back down or admit I was wrong. My mum and dad would try to tell me it was most often the *bigger* person who was brave and strong enough to apologise first – the one who could break the ice with a kind word. But I'd shoot them down and disagree, and it wasn't until recently that I realised they were right, appreciating that if you let anything escalate into an argument, you have to accept some of the blame, too. You're both wrong, in a way, if you couldn't calmly discuss something, so it *is* the bigger person who reaches out with an olive branch. You can be the person who brings the tension down a notch and calms the atmosphere, so that meaningful corrections and changes can be made. When you head in with an apology, a real conversation can take place. Trust stubborn me – it works!

Life is too short and there are so many bad, sad and mad things we all have to confront every day. So why not make every day easier by admitting we don't want to risk losing the people we love (or hurting them). Apologise, communicate, listen and move past a fight without aggression, with compassion. We all have rough moments when the world grinds us down, but let's do what we can to make those we love feel they are supported and nurtured and not like they are just another problem.

MY SUPERHEROES

Bradley Riches, twenty-two

Once I started seeing and accepting the positives of my uniqueness, that's when I started to thrive.

I am an actor and television personality, best known for being on Netflix's *Heartstopper* and

Celebrity Big Brother. I am also the author of a book called *A Different Kind of Superpower*, which talks about me being autistic and why it's a superpower. I've had to adapt to my life in a lot of ways. I love routine and order, and being in the creative industry makes it hard to have that control. But I wouldn't change my way of thinking ever, because my superpower helps me be creative and imaginative. Once I started seeing and accepting the positives of my uniqueness, that's when I started to thrive. Don't let anyone tell you that being different is 'weird' or 'wrong'. It's just YOU! Everyone is different ... but different doesn't mean less. The difference is beautiful. Neurodiversity is beautiful. We are human, and once you embrace your differences and yourself as a person, that's when self-understanding and self-love start. Love is an important word and means so many different things for me: the love for my parents; the love for my sister; the love for my fiancé; the love for my best friends; the love for my dog ... They are all love – just different types – and the one thing they all have in common is the feelings of comfort and safety they bring.

You've got a friend in me

Having good friends who care about me is one of my greatest achievements, and a true love story. As I mentioned above, I don't have lots of friends, but I'm a testament to quality over quantity, and I cherish each one. I don't need to be part of a huge social circle, asked out every night or included on every invitation list. I just need to be loved by those I love. The important things to me are the little check-ins: the text that asks if I'm well, or if something went my way, or sending love in a tough moment. I love it when my friends tell me they miss me, and I know it's true because I feel the same. Life gets in the way, but those little connections are glimmers of love that real friends can share in seconds. My best friend, Josh, and I don't need to text or call each other every day – we sometimes won't connect for two weeks at a time – but when we do, he feels like home, and we pick up where we left off. That's how you know someone has your back and is a loyal mate.

I met Josh when he taught me dance at university, and we understood each other right away. We got really close in my third year, and he asked me if I wanted to move into the spare room of his flat after I graduated. I thought, *Why not?* I moved in, then he met his partner, Ty, shortly afterwards, and they moved in, too. And that's how we became this trio of besties. My relationship with Josh was cemented because he was there for me so much – as my choreographer and as a cheerleader, when I was finding my way at uni and beyond, and Ty is just this incredibly motivating, wise figure who brings so much to my life. They are non-binary and they have taught me so much about life and love and embracing my differences and turning them into something powerful. After *Love Island*, when I decided to move in with Andrew, Josh and I couldn't live too far apart, so we still live down the road from each other and play an important role in each other's lives.

Friends should build you up, never knock you down. Josh made my confidence as a dancer blossom, even with my disability. He really guided me and put me on my path. He assured me that I shouldn't be afraid, backing up my dad's reframing of my deafness as a superpower. Ty walks the walk of combining confidence with humility and emits an amazing energy that has helped shape me into a braver version of the girl I used to be. It's so incredibly important to have these types of people around you – people you can turn to for a boost, a reality check or a hug. My friends are my safe space. If I'm ever feeling down, misunderstood or rushed, I meet them for dinner or go round to see them to chill and chat, and they help me through the tough times.

These are the people who feel like family – your framily. Everyone likes to feel appreciated, so think about who your framily are right now, and make sure you tell them just how valuable they are to you.

When you're sharing your limited, precious time and energy, remember that who you choose to be like family has nothing to do with blood. Your framily are people who give you support, motivation, love and courage. You find those people where you can, and cherish them. As I've said,

I struggled to make and keep good friends when I was at school, which I think has made me take friendships seriously. I had friends I'd hang out with at school and university, but they're not people who have stayed with me. Whereas the six friends I have now? We're going to end up in a retirement home together!

My new-found fame did change the dynamic of many of my relationships for a while. When I first got out of the *Love Island* villa, it was tough for those I loved to understand what I was going through and the public interest in me. I went from being an unknown model–dancer, to coming out of the villa and my social media profile soaring and being inundated with invitations to fancy places with well-known faces. My life flipped in an instant, and even I was struggling to keep up with myself and who I was. It got to the point where the internal fight I had going on between being the same old Tasha with family and friends and this whole new, shiny life in the spotlight got too much, and I burnt out. I broke down. I felt like I was losing my friends because I didn't have time to see them any more.

Communication was key then, too. I told them straight. 'Look,' I said, 'I'm dealing with a whole, new life after being in a bubble for six weeks. Give me a minute to stop feeling overwhelmed and get use to this new reality.' My lovely friends – and family – gave me the time and space I needed. And after a while the craziness calmed down and I settled into a more balanced state, where I could spend quality time with them. So that's another relationship tip: be upfront about what you're going through, and ask for space, time, a break, whatever you need – but say it with love and respect and assure them it's you not them, and it's a short-term re-adjustment plan.

Love is all around

I'm a very touchy person - in a good way - and I *love* love! I would say I'm a giver without any expectation of getting things back in return (although it's always nice when I do). Here's how I show affection:

- I like holding hands, giving a hug, feeling closer to someone by giving a gentle touch on the shoulder or arm. Nothing feels better to give or receive than a cuddle or kiss out of the blue. Physical contact breaks down boundaries, making it easier to share se-crets, worries and ideas.
- I love buying thoughtful gifts for loved ones and seeing the smile on their faces when they see what it is. Finding that perfect present is as much a treat for me as for the person I've found it for. It's true - it is just as

big a gift to give as to receive. Next time you see a little thing you know someone would love, treat them to it - even if it's not Christmas or their birthday - and note how excited you feel when you hand it over.

- I adore spending time with someone I care about, one on one, no big plans or prepping, just us being able to connect and catch up. I love a trip to the cinema, a dog walk with Luna, even just sitting snuggled together on the sofa scrolling through Netflix. Little moments go a long way and make a big difference. Make sure you leave space in your life for these moments.

- I enjoy making people happy and making sure someone is content and healthy, so I'll sometimes send cards with powerful words for no reason, just as a cheer-up reminder that they're loved.

- I celebrate the big occasions. When I was with Andrew, I made a scrapbook, filled to the brim with wonderful moments we'd shared so far, all our memories and letters and photos together. Gather your own tickets, letters and photos and make a book for someone special to you.

- I try to plan little trips to carve out quality time for people. I recently planned a weekend at Soho Farmhouse with friends and we got drunk and gossiped and giggled for forty-eight hours. Put something in the calendar with your besties, even if it's a year off from now.

Find your equilibrium

Balancing your personal and professional life is so important. You don't want to lose touch with either side of what makes you *you*. When I first got out of the villa, I was overworking myself and saying yes to everything that was offered to me – it was that work ethic my parents had taught me. But then I made myself look at commitments in a new way: does Project X or Y align with my values? Will Event X or Y make me happy? Would I rather be spending time with my parents or Josh than take on this new task? I stopped saying yes as a reflex, and reflected on what would be healthy for me and my relationships. It wasn't all about money – it was about values. I considered my long-term goals when I was offered the chance to work with different brands, and whether it would benefit my future. Finding this balance has been life changing and, tellingly, two years after *Love Island*, I'm still working with the brands it felt right to say yes to. That says a lot and reminds me I've done a good job of working out what is really important, both professionally *and* personally.

Write a Yes List

I think people are afraid to say no but, actually, we must. Try writing a list of who, where and what makes you happy and feel good. The things on that list are the ones you have to say yes to – the rest can be pushed to one side. On my list would be my family, friends, work that gives me purpose and gym time. (I need to go to the gym every day to feel my best, so I make time for it every morning – that's time for myself, getting mentally and physically stronger.) These are my YES items, which I value above all else. Consider yours when you're planning your days.

Love and loyalty

Loyalty is a tough one to value and practise. I know my friends and family are loyal because they have stuck with me through my bad times and difficulties with the media and online. They're not going to leave as soon as something goes wrong – they're going to be there and stick with me. It's so important to have that loyalty – and it is rare. There are those who will leave when things get tough; people you considered to be good friends who suddenly become distant for no reason or when you can't give them something they want. But one true friend is worth a hundred disloyal ones. So study your circle and work it out for yourself. Who isn't talking about you behind your back? Who doesn't ditch you when something more exciting comes up? Who checks in on you when you've been ill, down or received bad news? Mutual loyalty is the base of all good friendships. It's a sign of respect.

Fake friends

Coming out of the *Love Island* villa was a weird time because I did suddenly attract a few new 'friends' – people who pretended to be my friends but were really only in it for the short term. My core friendship group has been exactly the same before and since the villa, but I found that people I hadn't spoken to in years were getting in contact, and it worried me what their motive was. I always stay civil, but I know who my true people are and how wide I should make my circle. They are my priority over others that I haven't spoken to for five years who suddenly want to hang out since seeing me in the newspaper. I know exactly what's going on. It can be easy for some people to enjoy the attention from these new people in their life but I was determined not to. I got into a habit of thinking, *Would the person I met today have cared about the pre-*Love Island *Tasha – the deaf girl trying to make a living as a dancer?* I'd make myself remember what was real.

I know that people can easily get messed up by fame – drugs, drink. This was probably why my dad, in particular, was so nervous about me going on television. With his warnings in my mind, staying grounded has become a big thing for me. I have amazing opportunities, campaigns, parties and events, and the buzz is intoxicating. It can be easy to get swept up in the thrills and forget about what's really important: family, friends, your own mental and physical health. My family and friends have been key to my not getting lost in it all. They ground me. I come home to a safe space, and that is my reality – not the glamorous swirl in the outside world. Social anxiety was actually a big thing for me coming off the show, with all the interviews on the red carpet, shoots for magazines and constant attention. I was always worried that any one thing I said could blow up, and my new world would collapse. Ultimately you have to focus on staying balanced. And for me it's my family and friends. The other stuff is just noise.

My advice to anyone coming off the show is to take a break, take time out for yourself and remember your framily and the people who were there from the beginning.

Is there still love for *Love Island* ...?

Being on *Love Island* added another few weapons to my superpower arsenal for sure, which I'll always be grateful for. It
helped me build on my resilience. It wasn't the easiest of times
for me in there, not everyone has the perfect love story or experience. But I don't regret taking part, not for a single moment.

There are some people from the series that I won't stay in
contact with – purely because our lives have taken different
paths and the reality is that not everyone stays in touch after
the show, as close as you all are while you're in there for those
six weeks. I guess it's like a workplace – you don't always stay
in contact with colleagues, because life moves on. But then
there are some that I absolutely will – like Paige, who I absolutely adore. We have a great friendship. She lives in Wales,
so it's hard to meet up, but we're there for each other. Like I
say, everyone just goes back to their own lives and they have a
whole new life in the public eye to get on board with as well,
new friendships and relationships, career opportunities and
gossip. We're all going through the same thing, but separately
and at the same time. And that's probably good in a way. It
would be weird if we were still trying to recreate those six
weeks in the villa. It could never be real, so we'd be trying to
look for something that didn't and couldn't exist. It's healthier
to have no regrets and move forward.

Self-love is magical

You have to love yourself as well, right? And women in particular are really bad at that a lot of the time. So just stop. Love yourself:

- Don't be too hard on yourself if on occasion a yes turns into a no.
- Don't feel guilty if things slip down – or off – your list.
- We all get tired, ill or overwhelmed at times. I hate letting people down, but sometimes I have to.
- Put your own health and wellbeing first and be honest about it. Don't try to lie or hide what is really going on; we rarely get away with that.
- We always think about our friends or family or partner, the dog – whoever. But sometimes you do just have to love yourself a bit and give yourself a break.

Say no, say yes, say leave me alone, say give me a hug. And those of us with disabilities deserve everything, too. We are just as deserving of love, time, forgiveness and peace. We have earned every ounce of the love we show ourselves.

The first love we should all experience is of and for ourselves. Before I loved myself, I couldn't truly love anyone else in a romantic relationship. And you will no doubt be the same, even if you don't fully appreciate it yet. I used to expect that all the things I wanted would come from someone else when I was in love: validation, hope, security, motivation, passion – but I needed to give those things to myself first. Because before you learn to know yourself, and grow yourself, you can't choose the right partner. Self-belief and self-love are hard to acquire, and call for patience. So take baby steps learning what you value, want and need.

Reflections on self-love

Now, you might think this is a bit cringey, but I promise you it works, and I still do it now: every morning, when you're cleansing and moisturising or putting on your make-up, look at yourself in the mirror and say out loud one thing that you love about yourself, or something you want to achieve - and know you can - that day, or a positive affirmation. It really gets the day started on the right track. Or, if that feels too cheesy, buy yourself a pretty notebook, keep it by your bed, and write one positive affirmation or dream in it every morning. I dreamed of being on *Strictly Come Dancing* and I manifested it so many times in the notes on my phone. I just put it out to the universe and eventually it came

true. I was so happy, I cried so much when I
got the call.

A notebook can also be the place where
you reflect on what you've done in the past
and how you'd make it better going forward.
The power of the pen – it's real.

When life goes wrong . . .

Loving yourself and having some life-affirming daily prac-
tices in place can really help in hard or dark times. You can't
ignore trauma, try to hide it or push it away because it will
always come and find you. You have to go through it, head-
first sometimes, and feeling the negative emotions will make
you appreciate the nicer ones more. It requires courage – but
I know you can do it, once you harness your superpowers.
I've tried suppressing feelings and ignoring pain around my
parents' divorce, and it doesn't work. Rip the plaster off. Face
your fears and start the work.

The most important thing I've had during all my trials and
tribulations is my innate sense of self-worth. I didn't know
what it was, and I didn't call it that when I was a teenager,
but I knew deep inside me that I was destined for something
great in terms of using my platform. I always knew I had
value, as do all people with disabilities, and that at one point
in my life I was going to get an audience and be able to help

lots of people. It was just a feeling, but I've always had it, for as long as I can remember. Do you have a gut feeling that you can nurture, too? Perhaps a deeply embedded belief that you *can* sing, dance, paint, write, travel, teach, fundraise or whatever – no matter what other people tell you. Well, hang on to that self-belief. Cling on tight. Don't let anyone take it away from you. I'm not saying that proving other people wrong and loving yourself will be easy. Believe me, there are times when it will be very, very hard, but I know you can work hard, focus, learn and grow – I *know* you can.

All my life, I have set myself goals and worked hard to make them happen. I will look ahead: what do I want to achieve today, this week, next year? Through the hard times, I keep hold of my vision. And I love myself enough to know I can make anything happen.

Here's how to stay focused:

- Don't lose yourself in what's happening around you – all that noise is a distraction. Just keep focused on your path and the goals.
- Stay grounded. Having a quiet, conscientious faith in yourself is different to being arrogant. Let your achievements do the talking.
- When I have achieved a goal – that's when I get more confident, and my self-belief grows stronger. Use your successes as boosts of momentum.
- Some days will be tougher than others. Look in the mirror and say, 'I can do this. I can keep going.'

Baby steps are still steps. Not everything needs to be a massive goal. Sometimes just getting out of bed and showering takes a lot of self-belief.

- Eventually, I promise, you will get to a point where you feel invincible and that you can do anything you want to do. I love this for you and for me, but remember to stay humble and grateful, and keep acquiring new skills. You are never done. You are never perfect. But you will always be you. Make sure you remain someone who you can love.

Manifesting love

This is where I confess that I absolutely believe in our ability to manifest that which we would love to happen to us. I 100 per cent manifested the chance to go on *Love Island*. I would light candles and say to myself, I will be on *Love Island* one day – and it happened! I also manifested getting more TikTok followers with my friend Ty, and they have over a million followers now, while I have 862k, which is just incredible. My social community are amazing. It's all about what you put out into the universe, and then it's about thinking hard, working hard and making it happen. You can't dream a dream and hide in your bed believing you can manifest it into reality. Nothing in this life is handed to you. But manifestation is the belief that if you put the time and work into your goal, you can achieve it.

There are many ways to manifest your dreams: lighting a candle and meditating on a person or thing; making a mood board and placing it somewhere you'll see it every morning when you wake up; writing your wishes down in a notebook as you head to bed and imagining the outcome as you drift off to sleep. Find what works for you. Each act can be like a little check-in with yourself. And remember, it may sound crazy but truly, at its core, manifestation is just the self-belief and self-love we talked about earlier. The world truly can be your oyster – just think about it!

Embracing You

Five ways to love yourself to a powerful place

1. **Find your purpose.** I truly believe I was born deaf for a reason. I see it as a gift, and I'm so thankful for it because I can now use my platform to help others out there, something I love more than anything. I believe my purpose is to be doing what I'm doing right now, using my voice as much as I can. If you find your purpose, that will really motivate you and will make you so passionate about what you are doing. It'll keep you on track and you will have a strong vision ahead of you.

2. **Move forward, move on.** This is a scary one! I've gone through a lot of changes in my life, but I

believe they happened for a reason. Going from a small town – Thirsk in Yorkshire – to London was a huge change, but I knew I had to do it to pursue the career I wanted. I knew I was not going to flourish and grow in my hometown. I was taking a huge risk – but if it didn't work out, I knew I could always go back.

3. **Set goals.** I believe that setting goals is a great way to reach for the stars. No dream is too big! Although, when you are setting your goals, they can be small or big. Find what works for you, what you would love to be doing, and don't compare your goals to anyone else's or think you can't achieve something because you are 'different'. Your aims are personal to you, and only *for* you.

4. **Take action.** You can't expect the universe to do everything for you. You also need to put the hard work in, and it will pay off. It works both ways: whatever you put out there and give, the universe really does work in mysterious ways and will give back to you Give love, get love.

5. **Don't focus on the negative.** Nobody needs negativity. I don't like being around negative energy; it can be very draining and difficult to deal with. It goes back to putting yourself first, bringing love and light into your life. Cut out the negative and you'll feel a huge difference and relief.

chapter two

respect

We don't need to share the same opinions as others, but we need to be respectful.

Taylor Swift

Respecting yourself enough to set boundaries is a form of self-love; and respecting others' boundaries is a way of showing love. You should see a red flag waving in the distance when someone repeatedly refuses to stick to the deal you agreed to at the beginning of your friendship or romantic relationship. It should be expected that those you have allowed into your life respect boundaries and don't overstep them – that's how I see it. You deserve that. Everyone deserves that, no matter the challenges and obstacles they are facing.

At its very root, respect is about manners. Good manners, I believe, are part of a social contract of being polite, punctual and kind to those around you. And you should expect those things in return. They are the basics, surely? And they should also apply outside your relationship or friendship. For example, have you ever been out to dinner with someone who has been charming to you but rude to the waiter? That is such a deal breaker for me. Because I'm known from TV and have a lot of social media followers, I can attract people who may want something out of me and will lay on the charm – but if they bark at or ignore someone else? That's not on. Good manners cost nothing; bad manners can cost you everything.

I've been disrespected by people in the past – even family members – and I'll give them a second chance and an opportunity to hear why what they said or did was not respectful. But after that one lesson, the burden is back on them to be decent. I'm not going to keep putting up with anyone's nonsense. That's another one of my superpowers: knowing what and who is important. And it's only when you respect yourself and what makes you different that you can pull on that extra coat of armour and go out into the world, standing tall and dignified, a crusader for yourself and those around you.

How do you show respect?

I have a few rules set in stone when it comes to respect:

- Saying please and thank you should come as naturally to you as breathing.
- It is said that being late means you value your own time more than anyone else's. Aim to be punctual; and if you *are* going to be late, keep the person who's waiting for you informed.
- Don't be two-faced or suck up to the people at the top. On a shoot, I'm as respectful to the person clearing away the lunch things as I am to the photographer.
- Don't be the person who complains all the time. I hate it when I'm out if someone I'm with makes a big deal over a small mistake from a bartender or shop assistant. Everyone has bad days. Show grace and kindness.

You come across a lot of rude people in the industries I've worked in – modelling and television. Professionalism should come as standard, but it really doesn't. I've seen some people behave nicely to one person, and then awfully to another. I could never be that person. Plus, you never know who these people you're being dismissive towards know, or what they could be going through (everyone has hard times, even those who seem like they have it all).

Being polite goes a long way. When I hear that someone fed back that I was a hard-working professional on a television show, I feel as proud of that as anything else. The world is actually very small, and word gets around. If you're working in an office and it's noted that you're always late and you gossip about everyone, people won't trust you. Think about your impact on the world around you, and make sure it's a positive one.

Not letting people down is a big thing of mine. One time I was very, very ill, but I had a really big shoot booked, so I still got up and went because cancelling it would have cost them a lot of hassle and money. They respected me for getting through all the shots and giving them what they wanted, and I loved what they did. So there was lots of mutual respect that day, and because of that, I got to work with them again. Mutual respect is magical.

 My Top Five Songs about Self-respect

1. 'Titanium' by David Guetta, featuring Sia – this song gets me motivated and makes me feel invincible! If you're struggling on that last set in the gym, blast this one.
2. 'Hall of Fame' by The Script – this makes my heart feel safe and secure in a certain way ... like we all belong here!

3. 'The Saturdays Megamix' – a seven-minute combo of all their hits that really gets you going!

4. 'Summer 91 (Looking Back)' by Noizu – a summer banger that makes me appreciate the memories I've made and the achievements I've, well, achieved.

5. 'Never Say Never' by Justin Bieber – an old-school one, yes, but the lyrics are so meaningful, and the song is so fun, it never gets old.

Size matters

Don't discount the small gestures. Giving and receiving respect is such a simple thing to get right, but so many people get it wrong. I hope this chapter will work as a good reminder, especially for younger people, who may not realise that a simple thing like saying 'good morning' or 'have a lovely evening' when you work in an office can make such a difference. And more than that, good manners can even cheer up someone's day. They might be going through a hard time, and a compliment, a door held open, a cheery hello, can make the world feel a little less bleak. I'm quite a chatty person. I will ask a waiter how their day has been before I order a meal in a restaurant, or chat to Uber drivers about the traffic and how many pick-ups they've had that evening. I'll make conversation with someone waiting in a queue on their own looking a bit lost. Making those around me feel a little happier makes me happier. There are so many bad things happening in the world so we should all do our bit to be kind and respectful to each other.

Setting boundaries

Learning to say no is, in my opinion, one of the hardest things to get to grips with, but the greatest first step to self-respect. And a clear, decisive answer – even when it's no – saves everyone a lot of hassle.

We're so uncomfortable around putting ourselves first, or just being realistic about our time, financial or physical restraints – often agreeing to things we can't or don't want to do to avoid that awkward moment of refusing an invitation or a request. We've all been there, haven't we? I bet you've agreed to go out for a fancy dinner when your bank balance tells you it would be more sensible not to, or you've gone all in for a weekend away when you know you should be home resting or revising or getting ready for a busy week ahead.

You must get OK with saying no. I managed to do this when I realised that saying yes to everything that came my way was making me miserable. Some things you are offered, whether socially or professionally, just won't make you happy – and you need to get to know yourself (your interests, your passions, your needs, and who the people are who make you feel good), so you know when to say no, and can do so without feeling guilty or selfish or adrift in a sea of FOMO. Turning down work when you're freelance, like I am, is especially hard, because there's always that nagging fear that you'll never be offered a job again and then you'll end up with nothing. But over time, I've toned down the dramatic (and unrealistic) responses swimming around my head, and now consider logically: am I passionate about the opportunity? Do I have time for it? Will it further my career? I remember the first time I put these principles into practice with my management I was really scared. I told them that a particular project didn't align with me, and waited for their response. But they said, 'That's OK. That's what we're here for, to offer you things and help you decide.' Such a relief. I think often we build up saying no – and the effects it has on others – more than necessary. Perhaps we all need to remind ourselves that we are not the centre of everyone else's universe. The world can rumble on if we turn down a drinks invitation, a project, an exercise class . . .

Today, I'm at the point where I've turned down many jobs, and I feel good about it because I know who I am as a person and what I want my career to look like. If something doesn't align with what I'm doing, or if it doesn't make sense to me, I say no quickly and easily. I think it's good in a way because it shows I'm not just here for the money. I have integrity. When I do work on something now, it's because I love it or care about it.

Here are my five tips for setting clear boundaries:

1. Take your time before you commit to something
    that isn't an obvious and instant 'yes' for you.
    Better to think about it for a day or two than to
    regret your decision. Do always give an answer,
    though. Be respectful of someone's request or
    invitation and how you would expect them to
    respect one extended by you.

2. If someone steps over your boundary, whether it's
    making a rude comment, being late, wasting your
    time – whatever it is that pushes your buttons –
    let them know in a firm but fair manner. No
    hysterics, just a straightforward 'I'd rather you
    didn't . . . ' or, 'I don't like it when you . . . '. Most
    people appreciate a clear warning, rather than
    being ghosted or gossiped about.

3. Take stock. Are you too immovable in your
    boundaries? Could you loosen up a bit?
    Sometimes we get set in a certain way of thinking
    (often inherited blindly from our parents or
    upbringing), so it's a good idea to reassess your
    limits and your no-nos every now and again.

4. Accept a sincere apology from someone who
    overstepped your boundary – it's good for you
    to forgive. Everyone messes up, and everyone
    lives by different rules. If they overstep again,
    however . . .

5. And if you overstep someone else's boundary, don't be defensive – it's *their* boundary. If needed, apologise, change your behaviour going forward and thank them for their frankness. We all have our own irks and grumbles, just as we all have our own superpowers. Life is best lived when we all get along without stepping on each other's toes.

MY SUPERHEROES

Sophie Dove, twenty-three

We are so much harsher on our own appearance than others are with us

I struggled with multiple skin conditions – including acne and psoriasis – growing up, which means I've had to learn to embrace my skin for what it is and not compare myself to others. I've taught myself that having a skin condition makes me unique and since I changed my mindset my skin has become my superpower. My advice to others would be to remember that there is so much more to life than what your skin looks like …

and we are so much harsher on our own appearance than others are with us. People don't notice our scars and imperfections like we do, so embrace the little things that make you you! Choose self-respect. Show up as your true self every day and don't let anyone else's opinion change the way you embrace the world.

Feel the burn

Having that boundary around your yes and no answers is important because if you always say yes, you're going to burn yourself out very quickly. That's what happened to me. I got so burnt out after coming out of *Love Island* that even my dad and mum told me if I didn't set boundaries and kept going the way I was going, I would get so lost in my work and my image that I would lose myself and everything that was important to me. I was grateful for their intervention. I knew what they meant, and having them tell me confirmed my innate feelings around how I was coping with the sudden attention and offers. I look after myself so much better now, and if I feel like I'm going to get burnt out, I'll take a break and tell whoever needs to know that I'm going to go away for a few days or a weekend to refresh my mind, body and soul.

How does burnout feel?

How do you know when you're getting burnt out? Here are some of the symptoms I get:

- I get overwhelmed by even the smallest things, making me angsty or ratty.
- I feel exhausted, even after a good night's sleep. I go to bed tired and wake up tired.
- I get migraines, which make me want to hide away in a dark room.
- When I'm out and about wearing my cochlear implant, I feel sensorily overloaded – when I can't take noise, or crowds – and want to go home to hibernate.

Make a list of the things that push you over the edge. Note your emotions and fears around certain things in your calendar and analyse why you feel that way. And check in with yourself after a work meeting or night out with friends, or at the end of each day as you climb into bed, and work out: a) if you need that particular thing in your life or is it just too draining; and b) how you can get yourself back on an even keel. Sometimes just facing up to the feelings, and taking a few deep breaths, is enough. Other times, you'll have to adjust your boundaries to move forward without burning out further still.

Being deaf and wearing a cochlear implant makes my feelings of burnout worse, I'm sure. Even one event can tire me out for the whole week because they tend to be so loud. And even the briefest of conversations with someone requires a lot of lip reading. Multiply that by ten, and well, being sociable puts a lot of stress on my brain and my body. Conversation fatigue is a big thing for deaf people – concentrating on voices and lips when there's a lot of background noise is difficult. So it can get to the point where I'll head for the sofa and probably sleep all day. And that's OK – that tells me I need to stop for a little bit. Then I'll tell my management, without fear or embarrassment, that I've been feeling a bit burnt out and I need to retreat into my shell for a few days to get myself back to full power again.

There can be a stigma around taking a break or 'me time', especially when I complain and the trolls reply, 'But you're only an influencer, that's all you do . . . nothing!' But, actually, staying engaged (and engaging people) on your social media is hard work. You have to network, be social, produce content, say the right thing, share the right thing – there's a lot that goes into just one post. So if you're ever feeling the need to stop and breathe, please give yourself permission to do so – whatever people around you might say. No one knows your limits more than you. Please respect them, and respect yourself.

The four people I respect more than anyone

1. **My parents:** I have so much respect for them because they both started from nothing. They've worked hard all their lives to get to where they are now, they've never got lost in their egos and they've always stayed humble, which was such an important message to grow up with, especially with the life I have now. I'm so grateful and thankful; being around people like them teaches you a lot.

2. **Tyreece Nye, one of my two best friends:** Ty is incredible. Ty is invincible. Ty is non-binary and unapologetic. They always taught me to be strong and never be afraid of what strangers or naysayers say about you, and I sometimes wish I had their strength in terms of not caring what people think about me. I'm very sensitive and sometimes I really do worry and waste my energy on that one small negative comment, rather than focusing on the many amazing positive ones. Ty is working on that with me.

3. **Lucy Edwards:** she was on my podcast and what a woman! She went blind in her teenage years, and she just carried on with her

life and adjusted to her new way of being. She now uses her platform to help others and to normalise blindness. I have so much respect for her – she is unstoppable.

4. **Joshua Pilmore:** my other bestie! He was my supportive, understanding teacher when I went to university to study dance. When I was going through hard times in terms of chore-ography and my hearing, and getting angry at myself, he was patient with me, never once getting annoyed. He fully understood the struggles I had as a deaf dancer. He's the kind of person who will always check up on you and he puts others before himself be-cause he cares so much about his inner circle.

Escaping toxic people

Another really important way to show yourself respect is by getting toxic people out of your life. You know who I mean – the ones who put you down, gossip behind your back and are never happy for your successes or good news. These people are a drain on your emotional energy and will never change. Your success triggers them to feel jealous or less than, and that triggers them to be mean and nasty. It is not about you; it is about them. I'm telling you now: for your own peace of mind, you should only have people around you who lift you up and respect your time, your values, your qualities. Everyone else should be held at arm's length. You should remain civil and polite, but you don't need to have them in your inner sanctum, whatever they might try to tell you!

So how do you spot a toxic person? As I've got older, I've noticed that sometimes it's as simple as the vibe you get from someone when you first meet them. Some people just have bad energy, and you can train yourself to do a vibe reading: do they look you in the eye? Do they listen to your answers when they ask you questions? Do they gossip or talk negatively about other people? Are they constantly peering over your shoulder to see if someone more *worthy* has walked into the room? Are they rude to waiters or shop assistants? These are all signs that someone may not be a good person to have around you. But sometimes it can take months – even years – to see that someone gives off a bad energy; often, sadly, only after they've hurt you or let you down.

When I was younger, I had a boyfriend who was very toxic, but it took me months to realise it because he was very manipulative. Even when my friends told me they didn't like him, I was so hypnotised by his very deliberate charm that I defended him. Even when my friends told me they *hated* him, I'd reply, 'I love him; I choose him.' I was so blind I couldn't see how he was snaking his way into my affections and separating me from loved ones. I didn't know the signs and worked so hard for his affection. And he made me work hard, which, I suppose, reinforced the feeling that I was lucky to have him, that he could have done better than me. He refused to introduce me to his friends; he would never mention me on his social media. Even if we went on holiday for a week together, his posts would make it look like he was there alone. He wouldn't return my affection, yet he stayed with me.

There are always warning signs if you can keep your eyes open enough to see them, whether with a friend, a family member or a romantic partner. You need to respect yourself enough to clear your life of people who feel off, often on a visceral level. Give yourself back the power of trusting yourself: use your senses to know if someone is too gossipy, unreliable, bitchy or negative for you.

Self-protection is key

Being aware of toxicity in people around me has made me careful about who I share information with, and what I share. Some people can't keep a secret, or they embellish things to turn a half truth about you into gospel. Even when it comes to gossip at the school gates or around the water cooler in the office, think before you open your mouth and share your most personal thoughts and feelings. I'm very wary of oversharing. I stick to my family and close friends, and it can take a little while for me to trust someone. But that's OK – we need to protect our hearts and minds, so don't ever feel guilty about that. And don't be pressured to confess or share things when you don't feel comfortable doing so. Your feelings and thoughts are yours alone – you get to decide what you put out into the world. And only you.

I've been lucky and I haven't really dealt with too many toxic people in my life apart from that one relationship, a few school bullies and, of course, the countless online trolls (but I don't engage with any of them). Nowadays, I see the red flags. It's as if toxic people are waving them as they approach me – and I get the chance to stay clear. But it's harder when you're close to people – like it was for me with that ex-boyfriend – because the red flags get buried under love, and good people (like you and me) will always try to see the best in others. So it is really important to stop for a second, at a distance, and check your heart and head – and your gut – for those red flags. Take yourself out of a situation with someone who is rude to those they deem less important than them, or to you, or when people you trust, and have known for longer, try to tell you something isn't right. Protect your peace at all times.

When I came out of *Love Island*, there were plenty of toxic people out there, some who were definitely thinking about what they could get out of me. But what they weren't counting on was that I had self-respect and was in full self-protection mode and refused to suffer fools gladly. And I'll always be grateful to my mum and dad, and my few real friends for keeping me real.

Gut instinct – yours and your cheerleaders!

Sometimes I've ignored my gut instinct and then looked back and regretted it. Try to remember, you are your own best friend – or should be. What would you tell a friend who was in your situation? You'd tell them to trust their gut. And you should trust a true friend's gut, too. When I was in that toxic romance, I should have listened to Josh, who was saying to me, in a loving way, 'Tash, this isn't right. You're worth more.' But I ignored him and carried on with my nonsense. And of course, sometimes that is the way we learn – from our mistakes. We have to go through the heartbreak to know what real love is; we have to experience shit friends to appreciate the gold ones. Life is a learning curve. And it's a very steep one at times, but we have to keep going onwards and upwards.

Holding on to your self-respect on social media

Nowhere can drag your self-respect down quicker than the Internet, where it seems that anonymous nasties behind

screens are determined to pull people apart (especially challenging for those of us who think we are different or worry
that we stand apart from the 'norm'). How did we get so
spiteful? And isn't it sad?

Firstly, never engage in it – don't ever be that bully, for
that is what online trolling is, bullying behind a mask – and
then secondly, don't respond to it. Please know your worth;
and know that losers online are probably just bored, envious
or bitter. Their posts *about* you have nothing to do *with* you.
Here are some guidelines I use when I'm online to protect my
self-respect and to respect others out there sharing on socials.

- Think carefully about what you want to share. It
  will be around for ever, dug up before a university
  application or job position is considered.
- Aim to inspire. Do not aim to show off, gloat
  or make others feel bad. Try to bring humour,
  motivation, pretty views and tasty meals. There's a
  fine line between making people feel inspired and
  making them feel bad about their own lives. Before
  you post, think how you'd feel if those words and
  photos popped up on one of your channels.
- Search out the amazing people to follow and
  share the stories you know could help others in
  return. Maybe a bad-skin day, a belly bloat, a tiring
  experience at work, a moment of doubt. Bring the
  flaws *and* the fancy stuff. Connections in this crazy
  world are so important.

- Enjoy the creativity of social media. Make videos, take time taking beautiful photos, share inspiring poems or quotes, share book or film recommendations. Make your pages a place people can really dive into and be entertained by and use them as a place to really let your imagination flow. I love influencers who give out great travel tips and hotel suggestions, or those who provide interior-design and decorating advice.

- Obviously, you can make a career out of social media, which is what I do, but it's not easy – and don't believe those get-rich-quick tips that some dubious people post. As I've said before, it's hard work, takes time and builds slowly. You have to dedicate yourself to it and treat it like a real job. Because that's what it is.

- Relish the sense of community you can find online. Find your people. The world is your oyster. If you're lonely, you can find people who share your feelings. If you've moved to a new city or country, you can connect with those in a similar situation. You can find people in your industry to mentor you. I used to follow lots of professional dancers, for example, to get inspired by their regimes, programmes, choreography. We all need people to look up to and be included with.

Why respect can get lost on social media

The normal rules of respecting others when you're engaging with them in real life can get lost on social media, when people are behind a screen and forget about good manners. So, what do you need to be aware of when setting up a profile and engaging online? What are the cons of social media? There are a few, so you need to be aware of how private vs public you want to be with your world, how emotionally strong you are at any given time and if you can cope with negative engagement. And don't think for a minute that it's only people in the public eye who get trolled or have nasty things written about them on various platforms. Have you seen the comments section on blogs and news outlets? There's so much spite out there, so think about what you want to expose yourself to. Sometimes I think it would be more pleasant to just live in a little social-media-free bubble, but of course, it's now part of who I am, so I can't avoid it. Instead, I've had to learn how to handle it and here are some tips I've picked up:

- You *are* going to deal with that one person, that profile user 123456 who puts a hate comment on your Instagram or TikTok. How do you deal with it? You block, report, ignore – do not engage. They want your attention. It'll be tougher to handle it if it's someone you know – say, an ex-friend or ex-colleague – but the same applies: block, report and try to ignore it. This is really hard, I know, but take power from it – you've moved onwards and upwards but they're clearly still obsessed with you, spying on your page. You don't have to put up with their shit. You don't owe them anything.

- Don't feel less than because of the perfect lives and beautiful influencers you see popping up on your screen. We have to remember, it's not real life. It's not realistic. Successful social media engagement is about not comparing your lives to theirs.

- Check in with yourself and switch off if you feel overloaded. Being constantly on it could be really bad for you mentally, and can also steal valuable sleep from you. Before you know it, four hours have passed and you've been staring at a screen.

- You can feel like you are replacing real-life conversations or real-life interactions with social media as well. I sometimes feel like I've been super social and I'm mentally exhausted, but I haven't actually picked up the phone to a friend or been out. Social media makes us more isolated sometimes; in a way, it feels like it gives us the world but we're still just basically staring at a phone. Think about how you use your device in general, and maintaining respect for people when you meet them face to face. You have to be careful when you go out with your friends to not just stare at your phone. Look at the people you're with, talk to them, connect. When I go out with my friends for dinner, we have a new rule whereby we'll snap a photo, then we won't look at our phones unless we absolutely have to. I'm trying to do the same on holiday now, leaving the phone in my room for an afternoon or during lunch. It's about taking that time to sit, connect and talk to each other – because I don't want to be like those people who are just so deep into their phones that they forget about the outside world.

Be authentically yourself on social media

This is trickier than it sounds, but even in this strange, sometimes fake-seeming world, you have to be respectful of your true identity, ideas and ideals, and respect your audience enough to know they will know when you are not being real, even through their phones. It's hard because when you're trying to balance work stuff and personal stuff on Instagram, some people will relate and others won't; some will like your posts and others won't. But with a clear vision of what you're trying to do you won't get lost in the mess of other people's approval – you'll be doing things you are passionate about primarily for you, hoping to help or inspire others along the way.

For me, when I do little videos like putting my make-up on as I get ready for a night out, I talk about having a cochlear implant and having a disability, and I show putting my earrings on then my implant, and people can relate to that – making the most of what you have, lacking confidence sometimes – that sort of thing. Those posts I do always do the best for me, too. People appreciate what I'm sharing and know it's authentic in the context of me and my worries and my strengths. I like sharing on those posts, too; it actually boosts my mood to get things off my chest.

I do sometimes look at people's Instagrams and think, *Oh my god, their life and their relationship looks amazing . . . they have a yacht, a mansion, perfect date nights, and travel the world effortlessly . . . they do all these amazing things, and I'm unloading the dishwasher again*. But we have to remember to get back to reality and think that's probably not real all the time, is it? They likely work so hard to get that image out into the world, and it's doubtless very stressful trying to look perfect all the time. Maybe they're even battling to embrace a superpower they haven't revealed to the world yet, insecure about who and what they really are, but with kindness and acceptance they will get there. Now, I just post whatever I want, and I don't overthink it. If people don't like it, they don't like it. And if they do, hoorah – and that's why they choose to follow me.

Having a positive, respectful relationship with social media is about staying as true to yourself as you can, and if you feel you want to post ten photos of your cat or your dog, do it. I do – I love showing Luna off. It is one of the most authentic things I can do, to share my sweet dog with her floppy ears and cuteness. People may initially come to me for fashion posts, and I love those, too, but if you haven't been to my socials yet, expect lots of dog content.

A Parent's View

Tasha's dad, Tarek, explains how proud he feels watching his daughter turn her disability into a superpower, while not losing her good manners or respect for others

I remember watching Tasha at primary school in the playground around four years old, leading friends by the hands to go and play in a different area. This may sound insignificant to many, but to me it showed she had confidence, an ability to form friendships and maybe even leadership qualities.

Educationally, in the early days of Tasha not hearing, she was behind her peers in many subjects, but even back then she showed us she was prepared to try and fight to keep up, despite the challenges she faced. As Tasha developed, there were many things that could have knocked her back and kept her there: parents divorcing, the implant breaking, best friends dumping her, online bullying, lack of money, warring parents to name a few. These could have made her a different person, but with the love and support she received, and her own strength and mindset, she has remained respectful, humble, grateful, humorous, loving, considerate, adventurous, adaptable, courageous and ambitious. Tasha owns her disability, not the other way around. That in itself is a superpower. What gives me the most pride is the work she is doing outside her day job, in helping others – children and adults – going through the same struggles and

> *lack of confidence that she did; using her platform to*
> *educate and normalise disabilities. I am also extremely*
> *proud that she has not changed for the worse with new-*
> *found fame. In fact, she's improved!*

Being authentic is a big part of showing respect to others in my opinion. Liars and cheats don't respect you. Being decent, humble, polite and honest (with yourself and others) is the easiest way to get on in the day, and help you sleep soundly at night. Don't overthink anything – just do, say or share what feels right to you, and you'll attract the right people back in the long term. So many people get lost in a bid for perfection and end up losing themselves and their sanity. Don't do that – you don't have to. You, as you are right now, are strong and smart, bold and beautiful. Respect how far you've come already, and keep showing respect to those around you as you go forward and grow.

Embracing You

Five ways to replenish your sanity and self-respect

1. **Listen to music.** This is a really big thing for
   me when I'm trying to get back to a mentally
   strong place (see my list of tunes on pages 56–7).
   I'll put my headphones on and blast myself into a
   better mood.

2. **Light some candles.** I am big on candle love.
    What is it about candles? They can just change
    the mood of the room – and your vibe – instantly.
    They can get you in a calm and relaxing mode, or
    a citrus fragrance can wake you up.

3. **Give yourself a mental break.** I love to re-watch
    my favourite series on Netflix or binge a whole
    new show in one go. Get lost for a few hours,
    leave your stress behind and jump into a new
    world (you could even get some tips about self-
    respect when you observe what the characters on
    the screen are going through).

4. **Get to the gym.** It's not just a physical thing;
    it's also a mental thing. I go in there and do my
    thing, working hard, pushing myself to the limit,
    knowing that it will make me feel energised for
    the rest of the day.

5. **Bring some animal magic to your world.**
    Just going for a walk or sitting on the sofa with
    my dog, Luna, makes my heart happy. No one
    respects you like a dog; I swear – they look up to
    you, they worship you. Dogs are the best comfort
    whenever the world feels a little flat and you're
    not feeling worthy. If you can commit properly to
    a dog, I swear it will be the most loving, fluffiest,
    most devoted gift you can give yourself.

chapter three

growth

Becoming isn't about arriving somewhere or
achieving a certain aim. I see it instead as
forward motion, a means of evolving, a way to
reach continuously toward a better self. The
journey doesn't end.

Michelle Obama,
in *Becoming*

Are you the best version of you? Not yet, you'll probably say.
It's a good thing to acknowledge that personal growth is a
journey; to know that we never stop growing. That even
thinking for a hot minute we're done, complete, finished,
perfect is bad news. There is always room for us to learn
more, share more, make space for bigger and better ideas and
choices. I trust myself to make the right decision most of the

time; I trust myself to be a good partner, daughter, sister and friend. I'm not perfect – far from it – but I'm better than I've ever been, and that's what is important: to embrace who you are and to grow in the right direction.

The Tasha I am today is very different to the Tasha I was growing up. I've been shaped and formed by my experiences – some of the harder ones forcing me to grow up more than the nicer ones (moments in my life like the bullying at school and my parents' bickering and divorce). Being born deaf was the big thing that made me grow as a person, of course; from a very young age, I was in and out of doctors' surgeries, speech therapy, hospitals. Lots of obstacles were presented to me and my family that we had to jump over or fall at. I remember always being determined to jump. The biggest hurdle was during my A-levels, when my cochlear implant broke and I couldn't hear for a long time, which is so hard when you're supposed to be learning lots of new information at school and being social with your peers. Any free time I had then was taken up with hospital visits to get it fixed and sorted. That was a tough time mentally that will stay with me for ever. I couldn't hear for months and I was nervous about the operation to get the implant working again. But on reflection, I know that problem was put in front of me for a reason, and the reason was to help me grow – to become more adaptable, courageous and strong. We all have to grow from somewhere, and unfortunately in life there won't always be positive, good vibes surrounding us. You are going to have bad luck, but it's for a reason. It's for you to come back stronger. It's for you to grow faster. It's for you to look around you and become kinder, knowing that everyone, every day, is trying to get a foot over their own obstacles.

My Top Five TV Series to Inspire Growth

1. *The Traitors UK* – I *love* it! If you like a game show but with twists and turns, this is the one to watch. It's fascinating to see the cast get into their roles, interact and change.
2. *Echo* – a Disney show set in New York, which has amazing representation. The main character is deaf and most of the characters use American Sign Language but the majority of the scenes are relatable to being deaf in the UK.
3. *Sex Education* – I *love* this show, too. It's easy to binge but you learn so much from it about growing up and facing challenges. None of them has it easy.
4. *Empire* – this is about a family that has built an empire (money, power, notoriety) and it all comes crashing down at some point. Family is always there!

5. *The Summer I Turned Pretty* - on Amazon Prime, this is such a cheesy summer romance, but it's one to watch if you need some good vibes. The lead character is stuck between two brothers, and I love how she is on a self-growth journey. It's not just about finding a guy to love; it's about falling in love with yourself.

Reward yourself

Call it a carrot-and-stick technique if you want, but I'm always rewarding myself for a job well done. You should reward yourself after a period of growth as well. It's not a bad thing to do; it's motivating. I've noticed people are sometimes too scared to say, 'I'm proud of myself', but they shouldn't be.

In the past, it was standard for me to always be on the go, moving, changing, and I wouldn't stop for a second to reflect on how much I'd grown. That's a mistake. If we don't take a minute to feel proud and enjoy a well-earned reward (go for a long walk or two weeks in Ibiza), we can lose the momentum to keep growing. It was a big thing for me to introduce these moments into my life but I'm glad I did. Reflecting on and rewarding the distance you've travelled can boost your mood and make the struggles all feel worthwhile. You should always be proud of yourself, even the little achievements, no matter what they are, and even if it's only you who knows about them. Sometimes just getting out of bed – and making it – can be a challenge.

And it's important to know that it's OK if you don't achieve your goals, too. You can reward yourself for trying, and comfort yourself with kind words and something to perk yourself up. You may not achieve everything you want today, but tomorrow is a new day, next year is a new year. Even if you achieve one of five things on your list, that is a great accomplishment to celebrate and it shows growth.

Keeping strong and healthy

A big part of growth is physical. We need to stay healthy, strong and build up our immunity to face everything life throws at us. But we're not born knowing how best to treat our bodies, so how do we grow our healthy habits? How do we get better while keeping a balance between naughty and nice?

I've been through different stages when it comes to my body and how I treat it, some better than others. For me, obviously (because I used to be a dancer), I am trained to keep fit and enjoy taking care of my body, how I move it and my size. I grew up in the dance world loving to move, learning what to put in my body and, just as importantly, what not to put in it. I was actually very strict with my diet when I was at university, living on chicken and going to the gym every day during the week, only letting loose at weekends. That was too strict, looking back. I soon lost motivation and tired myself out. There were days – weeks, even – when I really struggled to go to the gym because I lost my mojo and couldn't stick to a routine.

MY SUPERHEROES

Josh Hughes, twenty-nine

My superpower is my Tourette's syndrome

My name is Josh Hughes, but some people know me as the Tourettes Barber. My superpower is my Tourette's syndrome, which I've had since I was fourteen. My TS came on very rapidly in my teenage years, and I tried to embrace it as much as possible, but there were days when it was really hard, and I just wanted to be normal. But as I got older, I came to terms with my condition and realised it's a part of my make-up … it's who I am, but I don't let it define me. I'm very lucky that I have a wonderful and supportive family who have helped me through the hard times, with an especially close bond with my sisters, Evie and Mia, who have always been my biggest cheerleaders. My fiancée, Lucy, and I have been together for twelve years and engaged for two. She has been on my Tourette's journey for as long as I can remember and has been - and always will be - my rock and beautiful voice of reason. I believe that life would be so boring if we were all the same, and I will always help and encourage people to embrace who they are. I've also learned to give less fucks about other people's negative opinions and surround myself with amazing, positive people. Tasha is a good example of a beautiful soul inside and out, who doesn't let anything stop her from pursuing her dreams. The word growth really resonates with me at the moment, as I'm trying to better myself as a person and grow in my business and career. Growth is a never-ending journey; we can always try to grow throughout our lives.

Then, on *Love Island*, I lost so much weight. You have to eat whatever food you're given, and it's quite basic – chicken, rice, salad, pasta – and pretty much the same every day, served out-side in the 40-degree heat. And I was just too hot and sweaty to eat. So when I came off the show, my friends and family were like, 'Oh my god – too much, Tash.' Then, of course, I jumped from that to being in a new romantic relationship, which is a heady mix of adrenalin and restless nights, going out all the time and eating and drinking too much. I eventually put on the weight I'd lost while recording the show – and I was fine with that. I was really happy with my body.

Where am I right now in my relationship with my body? I'm having a really healthy approach to the gym at the moment, and I've learned not to worry when my weight goes up and down a bit. I've put my scales away, and I like to *feel* good in myself, rather than tell myself a certain number or size means I've passed some kind of invisible test. That's a hard place to get to, especially for young women, but I know it's better for my mind to concentrate on how I feel, rather than what other people might think when they look at me. I'm careful if I have a big shoot coming up or if I'm going on holiday and want to look good in my bikini – but I do it for me. And I still treat myself to chocolate cake when I want it . . . or need it!

And that's my advice to you, for whatever it's worth. Try to love your good- and bad-body days, choose healthy when you can, both with your diet and your exercise, and treat yourself, too. Eat the rainbow, then go out for dinner with friends at the weekend and eat the fries. Don't cut experiences out of your life because you're always on a diet. Adapt. Notice what feels good in your body, and what makes you feel bad or fills you with regret. Accept that sometimes you will feel neutral about your body – neither positive nor negative, not feeling super-confident but not hating on yourself either – and that neutrality can be a position of power to do other things, to not focus on your outward appearance too much, and grow accordingly.

Fuel your fire

How do I grow strong and healthy? I'm a meal-prep girl! I love meal preps because they have all the nutrition and protein that I need worked out, easily available and easy to cook, and it makes me feel good knowing that I have put the right fuel in my body to grow strong and boost my immunity. Think about adding these winners to your diet:

- **Bananas** I love bananas because they fill me up as a snack and they are delicious. You can use them as toppings on your porridge or as a cheeky little sweet treat with melted chocolate. I love to treat myself. We all should. We all deserve it in these tough times.
- **Tenderstem broccoli** I love crunchy, delicious broccoli. It's good to get some greens

in your body and health is key.

- **Berries** Any and all. So tasty and healthy, I feel fabulous after having fresh berries first thing in the morning mixed up with natural yoghurt and some granola on top - absolute chef's kiss.
- **Sweet potato** I love to put sweet potatoes in a salad or even eat them as a jacket potato. They are so yummy, tick a sweet craving and they are very good for you and your body.

It's not just all about food, though. There's exercise, too. Think about how you feel after a yoga class or a brisk walk. A bit sweaty, but buzzing, right? Flushed and warm and ready for the day, or refreshed after a lunchtime session. I love to do weights at the gym and feel my power. Literally *feel* it. I love growing in my capabilities – lifting 10kg one day and 15kg the next. There are so many exercise plans, workouts, goals and schedules available to us now, whether in a gym or a class or online; when it comes to becoming fitter and stronger, there are limitless options. So find what works for you, and don't compare yourself to other people. Try not to secretly compete with their fitness journeys and just focus on your own, and what makes you happy, healthy and ready to grow.

Lose the booze?

I think many of us have toyed with the idea of sober living in the last few years, haven't we? Lots of celebrities are sharing their successes in giving up booze, and mocktails and alcohol-free drinks have got much better recently, too. It no longer feels boring to do Dry January or Sober October.

I've learned the hard way that alcohol can be the devil. I'd say that when I came out of *Love Island*, I was drinking a lot. Too much. When you go to red-carpet events, there's always free alcohol and lots of it, and I was drinking pretty much every single day. Plus, these same parties and events aren't as generous with the food, so the booze would hit quicker, and I'd go to bed hungry and feel rubbish the next day . . . until it was time to get ready to go out and start drinking at the next glam event. Once you are on a roll with the get-drunk-and-get-hangover cycle, the rest of your habits go downhill, too. You crave McDonald's or KFC. You waste the day feeling lethargic. You don't go to the gym . . .

That's why I decided this year that I needed to calm it down a bit and started off on the right foot doing Dry January *and* February. I had a word with myself and discovered I needed to stop leaning on booze. I can see now that when I first emerged into the public arena, I relied on it just to be sociable with people I didn't know or who I was slightly in-timidated by – having a glass in my hand made me feel more confident. Yet I could go out with friends and have a Coke Zero, while they drank cocktails, and be absolutely fine – I'd still have the best time and wake up the next day feeling fresh. So I noticed it was just in new or scary situations that I was using alcohol as a liquid crutch, and I think I got to a point where I was drinking to get drunk, just to be able to socialise and feel confident. Sometimes I used it to help me feel numb. Sometimes I used it to extinguish my emotions. Sometimes I used it to quash my social anxiety. And sometimes it turned me into a really emotional person who cried too much over very little. I never knew how it would affect me and that was discombobulating.

I've got a much healthier relationship with alcohol now that I've grown up a bit and realised I don't actually require it to have fun. Of course, on holiday, I'll still have a cocktail but I'm discovering I don't need it as much as I thought I did.

Everyone has different experiences with alcohol. People can be happy, angry, sleepy or up and down with it – it's very individual and the key is for everyone to know their own limits. Where is *your* full stop? When do you hit the zone where one glass – or one more glass – will stop you from growing into the person you want to be?

Don't let anyone get in the way of you saying no to booze. I've found that you can even inspire others to jump on the wagon with you. Maybe you have friends who have known for a while that they need to stop boozing, too, but felt the societal pressure we all feel to partake and didn't want to go sober alone. Ask around and see if any of them fancies trying it for a month (it doesn't have to be Dry January – any month will do), or even just taking a night off, rather than assuming you'll be sharing a bottle of wine. You'll all feel better for it and it can help to hold each other accountable. Going booze-free can be a great reset for a healthier life of goals, growth and good times without the morning-after-the-night-befores.

Coping with criticism

First things first: let's distinguish between criticism and feedback. Personally, I love a bit of constructive feedback. I built up a thick skin to this in my professions of dancing and modelling; both require auditions when you are looked up and down, your flaws and mistakes highlighted, with rejection likely most of the time. Constructive feedback has probably helped me to grow as a person more than anything else, and it's crucial to have people around you who will be honest with you and who you know have your best interests at heart – people you trust to share well-meaning thoughts on what you're doing wrong and what you could do better (preferably when such feedback is asked for!).

But how do you take that feedback, especially if you are sensitive about being different to those around you in some way? That's the next tricky thing. You have to *not* take it personally and realise that, in the case of auditions or job interviews, etc., what they're saying will help you to grow, so you can come back stronger. Show them you're taking their feedback on board, and that you *can* work harder and

turn some harsh words into a positive thing. If a dance in-
structor said to me, for example, 'Tasha, you need to kick
your leg higher,' I'd think, *OK, I'm going to go home and work
my butt off – then I'll come back and show you that I can kick my
leg higher.*

People can have so many opinions about you, and I find
the trick is to use that as motivation. *I'm going to prove
you wrong* is what I often think when I'm getting negative
feedback – and that immediately turns it into a positive. You
need to have a mindset of improvement and growth, rather
than one of surrender, especially if you go into a highly com-
petitive industry like I have. There will always be a hundred
other people waiting for your chance, job or opportunity, so
you can never rest on your laurels.

I want you to believe you're going places. That's how you
will keep growing and that's how you will prove what you
are capable of. Yes, taking criticism can be hard, but it's about:
a) how you translate it and b) not letting it hit you too deep.
It's how you come back from it that makes all the difference.
I'm here to remind you that you're allowed to leave it behind.
Throw it away. Move forward. It's within your power to do
with feedback exactly what you need to do. Sometimes I've
been given harsh criticism that I've decided not to let into my
mental space, and I've thrown it in the bin. And you can, too,
especially if you ever feel you have been criticised because of
your superpower specifically. If you're feeling strong, take it
as a chance to educate. But if you haven't got it in you at that
particular time, know that you are the bigger person, who

goes out into the world with an openness and empathy your critic clearly lacks.

Taking criticism – who to listen to and who to ignore

- Ask yourself: is this person coming from a good place where they want me to grow or are they trying to make me lose confidence or second guess myself? The more you can actually think about that, the more you'll know whether to take their advice or not.
- Are you being too sensitive? I'm quite a sensitive person, so if someone says something a bit harsh, I'll forget the hundred nice things they've said and just focus on the one mean one – and that one thing will wake me up at 2 a.m., worrying about why this person doesn't like me or that person doesn't understand what I'm trying to do (while they've probably forgotten they even said anything). Try to work out if you've blown a comment up out of proportion. I am actually reprogramming my brain to focus on the good stuff.
- That 1 per cent of negative people who are just there to annoy you, to get to you? They should always be ignored.
- Don't take criticism from anyone you wouldn't go to for advice. I admire my friend Josh, so if he said to me, 'Tasha, you need to work on this,' I would accept it because I trust and admire him. But I

wouldn't take harsh feedback from someone who doesn't have a clue about the area I'm in. And nor should you.

- Criticism on social media? Block, block, block. Honestly, straight away. Don't give them a reaction because that's what they want from you. They want you to feel beaten down. They want you to feel less confident. So it's about removing yourself from their negativity and bad energy. Block, and you won't have to hear from that person ever again. And remember, they're probably jealous at how far you've come – how you've grown – when they're standing still. Watching others flourish is hard for those who are stuck in the mud.

It's not you; it's them

I do understand that even negativity from idiots can get you down after a while, so in real life, avoid them, and online, use the special features to ban people, groups or words from your account. You can type in five words you want hidden on Instagram, for example, and posts or comments with those words will never hit your eyeballs again. Go to your settings now and give it a go. It works wonders for your sanity. It's like a virtual security blanket. I do feel that social media has become safer in the last year, and I hope it keeps going in that direction, with help from the government and police. But until it's perfect, train your brain to look for the good, be the good and numb yourself to the bad.

A Parent's View

Tasha's mum, Nicky, shares her tips on what parents can do to support a child with a disability and how that support will help them to grow, whatever cards they are handed in life

CONNECT: *We were lucky, as we had a great support team around us in terms of NHS care. The audiologists, parent liaison, the surgeons and speech therapists were very helpful and informative, and we also made an effort to meet other families in similar circumstances, too. We met other children with hearing loss, and this was good for me as a parent, but also for Natasha, so she could see other children wearing hearing aids and cochlear implants.*

FIGHT: *However, we did have to fight to get Natasha fully supported at school, which she needed. Her support came from a woman called Lady Mary Anne, and she was invaluable to Natasha's learning and confidence. She is now a family friend, and we owe a lot to her. Parents should not give in when fighting for their child to get them what they need. Get as much information as you can about what they – and you – are entitled to.*

> *MOTIVATE: Be proud of who they are and praise their achievements. Encourage and support your child to take part in activities. They are no different from others, so why shouldn't they? We also paid for Natasha to have weekly private speech therapy alongside the NHS sessions.*

Be your own cheerleader

We're all handed different blessings, quirks, opportunities and disabilities. You have to make them all yours – work with what you have – and have faith that you can grow. Go for it, grab life, and take the risks that come with that. I've got myself into a few very unexpected situations, and you will, too. Growth is about how you handle these in the moment, then use them to your advantage going forward. Trust me, there will be obstacles where things get hard, or slow, or draining, but I know you can push through the challenges, be present and be proud of yourself. And even if you fail, at least you tried – that deserves a pat on the back, too. And if life takes you in a different direction, that's fine as well. These days, it's so easy to doubt and hate on ourselves, but as long as you're working hard, that's all that matters.

Before *Love Island*, when I couldn't even pay my rent or my bills in London, and I was blessed that my mum and dad were helping me out a bit, I didn't get down or think how much easier my life would be if I went home to Yorkshire. Instead, I took on extra jobs on the side. You have to do whatever it takes to get to where you want to be. And with the right people by your side, and fire in your belly, you will add something to this world. You're here for a reason. You are here to grow, contribute and pull people along with you. Don't lose focus on your goals.

Embracing You

There's sunshine ahead

How can you stay positive, motivated and growing when you are going through a tough time, whether it's at school or work, or a bad relationship at home? *Believe in the universe and do the things that make you happy.* If you can take a holiday, read a good book or have dinner with friends and family – whoever you want to be with – do it. That's so important. Because if you don't have the things that make you happy, that's when you'll struggle on the day-to-day stuff, and that's where you'll lose yourself even more. Those little glimmers of joy and peace will build you while they ground you.

- **Try journalling.** You can keep the words to yourself, and no one needs to know about it, so you can feel completely free. It's a safe space where you can write your feelings down, then draw a line under it all and move on. Especially if you keep an actual diary – you can literally turn the page on today and move forward to tomorrow.

- **Seek out the lifters.** Socialise with positive people. It was a big thing for me when I noticed how negative people in my life were weighing me down, draining me, stopping me from growing because they'd stopped growing. Dealing with their negativity was keeping me small. And I'm sure you've come across people like that, too. But you know what? Sometimes you have to be selfish (although I don't really think it is selfish – it's self-preservation) and put yourself first. Refuse to be around people who don't want to grow or improve themselves or their situations, because they'll want you to stay in the shadows with them. You'll regret it in time if you keep those people around you, so cut them out – kindly and gently, of course, but remove yourself from their darkness. What will make you grow and do better is having amazing people in your life who give you positivity and support you, who nurture and nourish. And there really is no in between.

- **Have a purpose that's unique to you.** This will keep you motivated to grow. Because there's nobody else like you out there. Appreciating how special you are can really help you on whatever path you're on. Keep remembering that you're bringing something new to your platform, workplace, community or social circle that no one else has got. You are beautifully you, so you need to keep going – and growing – because no one else can do what you do!

I remember thinking once when I was going through a difficult period that I just needed to hang in there, to be patient and not lose my passion – not lose who I was at my core. Hold on to your value. You are priceless.

chapter four

resilience

Do not judge me by my success, judge me by
how many times I fell down and got back up
again.

Nelson Mandela

How do you handle the tough stuff and pick yourself up
when you've fallen over? You're back to square one (or
worse), possibly for the second, third, hundredth time – but
somehow, you've got to find the strength, power, resilience
to give it another shot. You might be overwhelmed, tired,
emotional, disappointed, betrayed, sad, but you can't let
it stop you. You can't give up. And you know what I've
learned? It's the biggest moments of failure or fear, when
you have to summon up bucketloads of grit from within,
that will make you invincible. The tough times make you

tougher – in a good way. Resilience is perhaps the greatest thing to come from whatever superpower you've been given in life.

How have I learned to handle life's hiccups? The most memorable moment for me when my resilience had to kick in was that horrid time in Sixth Form when my implant broke, and I was rendered deaf for months. I had A-levels coming up, a dance show to perform in and I remember being hit with an emotional punch: a visceral force yelled from deep inside me that I had to carry on. I clearly recall saying to myself: 'Do you want to hide away? Do you want to stay at home? Do you want to fail? Do you want to slump around feeling sorry for yourself?' And I answered myself: 'No! There will be so many more opportunities in the future if I keep calm and carry on *and* I will get a good lesson in how not to be rattled when things don't go my way.' So I still went to college, I still got on the train (and it was in Wakefield, so it was about an hour and a half to get there, and an hour and a half to get back – a draining journey), I still went to my dance classes and participated in all of my life as much as I could. Obviously, I couldn't do singing lessons because I couldn't hear myself, but that was the only thing that I couldn't fight. I look back on those months as being massively beneficial. I knew after that trying period that I'd be able to cope with anything in the future. And that's the first time I remember summoning my resilience – another superpower for my arsenal if I could harness it.

My Top Five Songs About Resilience

1. 'Stronger' by Kelly Clarkson - a great one to listen to if you're feeling down.
2. 'Firework' by Katy Perry - the lyrics are so relatable and it's a strong, uplifting song.
3. 'Greatest Day' by Take That - could there be a more perfect song to listen to at the start of the day?
4. 'The Climb' by Miley Cyrus - the best song about how life can be a difficult upward ride, the journey can leave you exhausted, but the views are great.
5. 'So What?' by Pink - all about having an attitude, but in a positive, I-can-do-it way!

Train your resilience muscle

During that time in my teenage years, I remember I wanted to go out with my friends, one of whom had a big birthday to celebrate, but I knew it would be hard. I had a dilemma: do I go when I know everyone around me will be having conversations I'll be left out of, or stay at home and feel sorry for myself, drowning in FOMO? You can guess what I did, I'm sure. I pushed myself to go for one hour, and people understood that it was difficult for me to converse. I lipread as much as I could, but it wasn't easy – it was exhausting – and I still felt a little left out. But again, I felt stronger knowing that I'd made myself do it, that my friends were happy to see me and that I didn't have to rely on my implant to be part of their world. That was a useful lesson because one day the implant may stop working permanently, or the side effects may get too much, or physically, things may deteriorate to the extent that I am fully deaf again – and I'll remember that night out as a teenager and trust myself to make the best of a bad situation as I did before. I think of that blip as an obstacle to prepare me for the future. It happened for a reason – perhaps many reasons.

When you are faced with a hard time or a tricky situation, use it as an opportunity to train and strengthen your resilience muscle. Challenges are important. I remember setting myself little tasks at the time – asking questions in shops, starting up conversations at the bus stop, seemingly insignificant things like that. But each tiny mission accomplished grew my self-worth and resilience.

MY SUPERHEROES

Meryl-Anne Williams, twenty-seven

If we all looked the same it would be a very boring world

My superpower is having dwarfism. I have a type called achondroplasia, the most common type. It means my arms and legs are a lot shorter than an average-height person's, but my torso is the same height as everyone else's. I never let anything stop me. I always say: I might not be able to do it the same way as everyone else, but I can do it my way, which is a bit different. Having my condition means I am constantly adapting myself to my surroundings, as the world is not made for me. Advice for others on how to embrace their differences? I always think that if we all looked the same it would be a very boring world. Your superpower is what makes you different from everyone else, so I always say to embrace your differences, as they make you unique. Resilience is a key word for me. I never give up and always keep on trying. Even if it does not work, I'll say if there is a will, there is a way.

Born this way

I've been asked if I feel I was born with resilience or if I had to gain some grit because of being deaf. I think it's nature *and* nurture. I would say a sense of resilience has always been a part of me, or that certain obstacles have brought it out of me naturally, but also that it's a learned behaviour, too. Over the years, I've seen my mum and my dad work hard, getting up every morning and putting others before themselves, facing different challenges, and I've picked up the tools they use: humour, kindness, honesty.

Don't get me wrong – sometimes, even with self-belief and great role models, there will be days when I really do struggle to even get past the point of 'Can I do this?' I bet you've been there too, right? I doubt myself sometimes, that little voice inside my head saying, 'No, don't be daft, you can't do it!' Sometimes that negative voice is an alarm, warning you of something dangerous or foolish, but more often than not, it's just fear or past experience climbing into your head and mucking you about. It can be hard to remove it – I've had to literally train myself to ignore it. And you know what I've learned to do? I tell that little voice to shut up: 'I was born deaf, I was badly bullied, I struggled with my parents' divorce, who am I to have a platform, to pose for fashion shoots, be at fabulous parties with famous people? I'm not worthy . . . SHUT UP! I *am* worthy.'

Try it next time you question your power. Tell that doom-and-gloom merchant hanging about your head to shut up. Scream it! Slam the door shut on that voice in your head telling you that you're weak. It's like having an angel on one shoulder and a devil on the other. But please, I urge you to listen to the angel – she'll bring the sparkle and magic you deserve.

A Parent's View
Tasha's dad, Tarek, on what parents of children with disabilities can do to support and keep them resilient

My advice is all dependent on the severity of the disability and the age of the child. However, there are some common strategies based on the fact that not all communication is verbal. It is fair to say that all parents-in-waiting expect and hope for that perfect child to arrive into the world. So the mindset of the parent has to be adjusted to a level of acceptance before any strategies can be put into play. Discovering your child has a disability is traumatic, worrying and emotional. I remember Tasha's mum and I cried every night for what felt like weeks before coming to terms with it and making a plan. In some ways, it was kind of a grieving process we went through – but in reality, looking back, it was wasted time worrying about something we could not change. Get the tears over and done with and make a plan to positively impact your child's future, rather than dwelling on what cannot be changed:

- *The help you give your child as a parent will build their self-confidence, their belief in themselves, their communication skills and their outlook for an optimistic future – their resilience. You are the teacher with the largest responsibility. It cannot be left to your child's school or social-services support. Most of the work has to be done at home. Pick up the baton and run with it as fast as you can.*

- *As they get older it is important to talk to your child about their disability, but it is more important to focus on the 'ability' part of that word. Instead of using terminology that mentally restricts them or instils fear that they cannot achieve, use positive language such as, 'You can do . . . '. Children will naturally compare their lack (in their minds) of ability to their peers', leaving them feeling inadequate or 'different'. Keep reinforcing the ability.*

- *Help your child to express their needs. Let them come up with their own solutions that will help them, rather than forcing yours on them.*

- *Join support groups with other parents whose children have the same or similar challenges. You will be amazed at the practical help you can gain from others who are in the same situation but have different perspectives, strategies and ideas you may not previously have considered.*

- *Be patient! Children with disabilities go through the same challenges of growing up, including going through puberty. That's hard enough for children without disabilities but, with the concerns they hold deep inside about their situation and their uncertain future thrown in, you must be patient and keep constant, open communication with them.*

- *Encourage their talent and interests. Help them to do*

something they enjoy or something that they can lose themselves in. This could be as simple as reading books to dancing. Do it with them. I danced with Tasha to the Steps Gold DVD, until it didn't work any more! We would copy the moves and she could feel the bass of the speakers through the floor. We had fun, she learned, she laughed, she found a talent that became a career.

- *Put yourself in your child's shoes and do what is necessary. In Tasha's case we immediately enrolled in sign-language classes, bringing Alex (Tasha's brother, who, at the time, was around nine years old) with us.*

- *Lastly, look after yourself. If you are not firing on all cylinders, you can't help your child be the best they can be. You need to build your own resilience, so you can help them build theirs. If you need support, reach out for it. Talk to your friends and family and use the support groups mentioned above.*

Duvet days

Having said all the above, it's also OK to occasionally admit defeat and take a break from being resilient, wonderful you. Sometimes it's hard to get up and at it; sometimes you need a day hunkering down under the duvet or hibernating in front of the television for a Netflix marathon. Cheat days are fine, and so are those times when you don't want to be strong – when you just want to feel safe. You don't have to always be on the go. Listen to your body. Listen to your brain. Again, listen to your gut. Hiding yourself away once in a while, until you feel more able to cope with the world, could be good for your mental and physical health. I'm not saying you should shy away from challenges or avoid hard tasks; just that it's not your job to fight every battle or be on it 24/7. Learn to distinguish between lazy procrastination and a genuine need for rest or escape.

I've found that women especially can be hard on them-selves, putting themselves through so much for their work or their families. And we have so much to deal with – periods, pregnancy, perimenopause and the hormone fluctuations and annoyances that come with all that. That's why it's so important that if you're starting to feel tired, you give in to what your body's telling you. If you ignore it, you'll get burnt out. So if your body needs McDonald's and *Bridgerton* and no phone or laptop time today, go to McDonald's, watch *Bridgerton* and leave your laptop and your phone on silent in another room.

How to handle rejection

Ah, this is when your mental resilience will really be tested: when you're being told no, or being dismissed, or being told you're not good enough. How do you get back up from that? In my life as a model and dancer, I've had a lot of experience in all the above. When I started out in my career, I knew I would go into dance auditions and face a lot of rejection before I got my first job, and I probably heard at least five 'no thank you's before I got my first 'yes'. But through it all, I did not take anything personally – I knew it was because the choreographer needed a certain look, or type or expertise; it was never because he hated *me* or *I* was awful. You have to take yourself out of the equation, basically. The dance industry is especially like that – they want brunettes not blondes for a job, or dancers under 5'5", for example, and you just might not fit the brief. And that principle carries across many professions. So try not to question if you're good enough. You have to keep going and not give up . . . and the rejections make the wins even sweeter. My first 'yes' was a contract to dance at a ski resort in France for six months, which was the most incredible experience and I had the best time. But who knows – if any of the many noes had been a yes, I wouldn't have got to do that. With hindsight, I knew I was meant to be there, with those people, at that moment in time.

That's how I started to think about modelling jobs when I got into that, too. I'd go to castings and get a lot of rejections. It took me a year to get any work. But I kept plugging away, refusing to doubt myself. Instead, I'd spend the time updating my portfolio, taking new pictures, trying different angles, styles and poses, putting myself out there for casting directors to see. The rejection you get in modelling is hard because it's literally on what you look like, which is tough for a young girl. But again, I'd disassociate myself from the job. Maybe they wanted a stronger brow or dark hair? I'd just keep telling myself to love myself because that's what truly matters. If you love yourself, you can get past any external judgement and through anything you choose to do. You feel like a fighter who has pushed the rejection away. Don't fall into a hole of hating yourself.

Then of course on *Love Island* there is rejection from the opposite sex. It's part and parcel of the show, not everyone is going to fancy you. I had quite a good experience in terms of getting to know people there, but inevitably there were guys who weren't interested in me because they only liked brunettes, for example. It could have felt upsetting but, again, I had to remember it wasn't about me – it was about what they wanted. Sometimes things can feel personal, but they aren't.

You can't make someone fancy you, or love you, or want you . . . they're saving you time and revealing they are not the person for you because they don't see your true value. You'd be getting yourself into a toxic situation with no long-term value. I've seen it play out in the real world a million times. Yes, we might have to kiss a hundred frogs, but eventually, we will find the right person – even when you're being filmed if you're lucky. Andrew and I got to know each other slowly but surely, probably in quite a boring way for viewers, but in a way that worked for us in our relationship. We let our relationship come to us over the weeks, and that would always be my advice: don't chase it or beg for it; let love come to you. It's best to keep love natural, rather than forced. Sometimes it won't happen with who you want or when you want, and you have to live with that. I didn't have to force anything with Andrew. We were put together as a couple from day one, but we ebbed and flowed, pushed and pulled, while a natural attraction kept bringing us back together. We realised a few weeks in what we were doing – maybe there was even a sort of fear because we felt something so strong for the first time ever – and agreed to just be together, ignoring everyone else in the villa. It was clear we really liked each other and had something worth focusing on, despite it not making the most explosive television. Looking back on the show, I'm so thankful I took the time to get to know all the men in the villa; I wanted to utilise the *Love Island* experience as much as I could – but I couldn't resist the magnetic pull that kept leading me back to Andrew.

How to beat the bullies

The toughest bullies I've ever come across are of the cyber variety and, if you are unfortunate enough to come across one, they will test your mental and emotional resilience, believe me! When it was happening to me at school, I felt ashamed that I was being singled out and was actually too scared to tell my parents about it. During that period of my life, I never knew what to expect when I walked past a group of people or checked my phone. The adrenalin and cortisol that rushed my body were awful. Simply trying to get through the day was the hardest thing, dreading Monday mornings, then longing for the three o'clock bell to ring.

I used to come home from school and be really quiet and subdued, so my parents knew something was happening. Then, eventually, after being withdrawn for months, it got to a point where I just couldn't bottle up my pain any longer and I let it all out. My parents were kind and understood, despite cyber bullying not having been around when they were teenagers, and they united over helping me. They both told me, unequivocally, that I should not be dealing with this, and complaints needed to be made. I said that I was scared to talk about it to anyone in authority because I feared a backlash, and that my life would get even worse. I wanted to keep going into school, trying to get along with these nasty people and not rock the boat. What my dad said to me as I explained this was crucial then, and an essential rule for us all to live by: it's important to speak up, using a loud, clear voice, for what is right – not only for you but for others around you who might also be scared or fragile. 'This bully or bullies could be making other students' lives hell and you don't realise it,' he told me. And his logic clicked with me. I realised I shouldn't be crying in bed because some keyboard warrior was bitter or jealous or just plain miserable. I shouldn't be scared to go to school, imagining everyone sniggering about some lies or gossip written about me online.

The worst part of cyber bullying is not knowing who is behind it; never trusting anyone, always looking over your shoulder. Anyone who's been bullied like this, even had just a few nasty exchanges, will know what I mean. You're on constant high alert.

I gradually learned to do what my dad said to get the better of the bullies. Here's some advice:

- **Speak up.** Please don't be scared to speak to your support circle, whether that's your friends or your family or even someone at school or in the workplace – a person you can trust and have a relationship with. They will be there for you and they will get you through it.
- **Take action.** It's scary, but taking action to prevent it continuing, or moving on to someone else, is the right thing to do.
- **Put yourself first and know this is not about you.** Nor is it about anything you've done. It's about the perpetrator. So take the weight of guilt or secrecy off your shoulders and you will feel so much better. After I told my dad and mum, and they went to the school head teacher who sorted it out, my life got calm again. I started going to school and being with my friends again without having to worry about anything.
- **Learn from it.** It was a challenging time for me, but it made me empathetic, kind, strong, and it made me want to get the last laugh. And believe me, I have.

The power struggle

I believe that in any walk of life, wherever you come across them, bullies are mean because they want to have power over you. They want you to be fearful, nervous, scared; they want to manipulate you. Ultimately, they want to take your power away from you. But they don't know you well enough to know you have your very own superpowers. You are resilient. You are strong enough to let it go. Look at them with sympathy – because you know you will have more grit and determination than they ever will. And they cannot take your power because it is woven into every fibre of your being.

I look back today and think, *Why did I waste so many years and tears on those bullies?* And I also feel lucky that I had my parents and teachers looking out for me. Without that support, I think I'd have massively struggled. Don't be afraid to open up to your family, teachers or bosses. My school was really good; they took action straight away, and the police got involved and eventually found who was behind it all – this one sad, small person sat at home, apparently obsessed with me, rather than making their own life better. Writing nasty things about me was how they chose to spend their time; not going to the gym or to the cinema, or reading a great novel – no, staring at a screen filled with mean words. It's so odd, isn't it?

Inspired resilience

I'm sure there are people in your life who have been through a lot and, to your amazement, have kept going whatever life throws at them. How do those people make you feel? Inspired? Motivated? A bit flat? Are your problems even real compared to theirs?

Firstly, it's important to remember that you shouldn't compare your life with anyone else's; life is not a contest. Secondly, don't let strong people dampen your resolve; let them water it! I have met people who have had to struggle with the worst things imaginable happening to them, or their loved ones, and I use them as mind mentors – as examples of people who keep going, keep growing, never allowing their misfortune to make them nasty or bitter.

Look around you and find your mind mentors – those you can call up or message for a pep talk or a few wise words when you're full of self-doubt or lacking strength, or just people to follow on social media who you know to lead by example, and whose page will fill you with fire. One of my greatest ones is Ashley Cain, the former footballer turned campaigner. He's with the same management team as me and we actually met for the first time at their Christmas party last year, but I'd followed him on Instagram for quite a while before then. He had a beautiful daughter who was diagnosed with an aggressive form of leukaemia at eight weeks, and died at only eight months old. The most heartbreaking thing, and every parent's worst nightmare. In the time they had together with their child, he and his partner brought her home and tried to spend her last days together, happy and making memories. I can't imagine, can you? The agony.

It's not only how he and his partner conducted themselves during that worst of times that amazes me but after, too. They set up a charity in their daughter's memory, The Azaylia Foundation, to raise money and awareness to fight childhood cancer. He challenges himself, pushing the limits of what he is capable of in honour of his baby girl: his recent challenge, Ultraman 2024, involved running, cycling and kayaking the length of Great Britain three times in three months. He's got so much resilience and just keeps going, using his grief to inform others, raise money and make people who have been through similar tragedies feel less alone. He puts himself out there when it would be easier to hide away and suffer in silence. When I got the chance to speak to him at that Christmas party, I was in awe. I told him I thought he was incredible, for taking the worst thing that ever happened to him and turning it into a positive for others. And for the fact that he gets up and dressed and carries on every day for his daughter, the sweet Azaylia Diamond Cain. He is resilience personified.

Make your bed

What so many people go through, often silently or secretly, and still get up in the morning – it's remarkable. We never know what pain and sadness those around us struggle with and still go out into the world kindly and gently, wishing well to those around them. I think we need to think more about these private battles – to make us more understanding as we wander the world, interacting with others, and to help us learn about resilience and what it looks like in the everyday. When I've watched Ashley doing all those amazing challenges, I'm like: I can do that, I can be strong, whatever life throws at me. I can choose to get up, be good and grow. Seriously, the way he conducts himself even gets me to the gym – thinking about the physical challenges he took on while dealing with so much mental trauma. He's a really good person in the public eye to connect with on social media if you're looking for motivation. Following people like him is a reminder that you can get through the worst crises and keep living a life of value and joy.

If you feel your resilience is sliding away and your bed or sofa is a safe space to hide away from the world and ignore your goals, challenges, problems or dreams, that's OK. Acknowledge that headspace, allow your mind and body time to rest, ask for help from those you trust and then seek out the mind mentors, the motivators, the Ashley Cains. Then wake up, make your bed and know that each day is a new day, bringing with it another chance for your resilience to show up. You can do whatever you set your mind to, I promise.

Embracing You

Five practical activities to restore your power
and build your resilience in tougher times

1. **Go for a walk.** Fresh air really does reset your mind. Sometimes being stuck inside all day can be draining, but going outside and getting that light and air will boost your mood.

2. **Try manifesting.** I do this as much as I can, and I love to treat my journal as my best friend because it's private and I can tell it all my secrets! Write down your emotions, goals, affirmations, and the universe will work in its mysterious, amazing ways. When I write down my goals, I write them as if they've already happened – like they are real. Put all your desires out there and believe in yourself enough to make them happen.

3. **Listen to music.** Whenever I'm feeling a bit down, I like to whack on my favourite tunes, cringey throwbacks that I can sing and dance along to. This gets me in such a great mood it takes my mind off anything negative that's been lurking in my brain.

4. **Switch up your mindset.** Think about other inspiring people you know who are going through tough times, and reach out to them. Form a community that uplifts and motivates you.

5. **Have a good sob.** This might seem weird but hear me out. Having a hearty weep is too often seen in a very negative way. I am a sensitive person, so crying is a good release (especially on *Love Island* – you may have noticed I cried a lot) and is how I deal with my emotions. I feel instantly better after a good cry. Often, it's better to let it out than bottle it up and explode in anger or anxiety or fear.

chapter five

change

The greatest discovery of all time is that a person can change his future by merely changing his attitude.

Oprah Winfrey

Are you good with change? It can be a double-edged sword, can't it? On the one hand it offers opportunities, new ideas and a refresh, but it can come with a side order of anxiety, fear and self-doubt: are you too set in your ways? Are you good enough to take on these new processes? Brave enough to meet new people and be chucked into unknown social circles? Whether it's changing school, job, city or country, getting married or ending a relationship, making a change can feel daring and bold. Again, trusting your gut is probably the first step to knowing if a certain change is for you.

I'm a firm believer that the only way you can grow is to change. Moving to London was definitely the biggest change I have ever made, and was all the things outlined above – the positive and the negative. But I knew, deep down, at a visceral level, that while it was a risky change, it was one worth making. It was a big thing for me, a small-town Yorkshire girl heading down to the big city. I went from living in a place with a population of 5,000 to a place buzzing and brimming with millions of people. I remember being floored by all the tall buildings and how big and busy everywhere was. The Underground was madly confusing, and I had many a nerve-wracking moment fearing I'd get lost or simply swallowed up in the chaos of it all. And I loved every minute! Luckily, I already knew Josh and Ty so I moved into a flat with them, and the most exciting chapter of my life story started to be written. I feel that moving to London was the change that started my life. If I'd stayed in Thirsk, my career wouldn't have taken off, and I know I wouldn't have grown into the woman I am now. I'll always be thankful I made that change, because it was in London that I felt empowered to live authentically and be myself for the first time.

I really do believe that the universe pushes things in front of you and dares you to take the challenge. You have to make changes in your life, in your career, in your relationships, if you don't want to stay static or be stifled. Things that don't make you happy need to make way for things that do.

The Covid lockdowns gave us all a manifesto for change

on a nationwide and global level. Do we need to work in an office and commute? Should we spend more time walking in nature? Do we need this bigger social circle or would a smaller group of trusted loved ones work better for our mental health? We had the time and the impetus to take stock, and many of us have kept the changes enforced on us during those discombobulating times. Even having to deal with not going to the shops or the gym forced us to change how we cook and consume or work out. It made me much more self-sufficient. We were all massively impacted, and while some of us are still dealing with the negative changes those months imposed on us, I do think it was an interesting experiment in being made to change our ways and judging the outcomes. The younger generation in particular had to deal with a lot of changes – the arrested development, the curtailed social life, working from home, learning from home. I feel there's been an uptick in social anxiety because we couldn't go out and live our lives as we had done for so long. But going through it, trusting in the universe and coming out of it has been the biggest societal change in my life, and again, I'm so grateful for the lessons it taught me. Yes, both moving to London and coping with Covid taught me how to handle change, expected or not.

MY SUPERHEROES

Jessie Yendle, thirty-one

You're never alone

I'm a full-time content creator and ambassador for people who have a stammer, but I've also recently developed a tic disorder. I've adapted my life, working to overcome my struggles … like the fear of phone calls, drive-thrus and just speaking [to people] in day-to-day life. I've made it work by building my confidence from the ground up. My stammer is less the more confident I feel. My advice would be to OWN your superpower and realise there's a whole community out there, many others like you! You're never alone. I feel the world is more exposed to all the different superpowers out there thanks to social media and the people who are spreading awareness. The day will come where you'll hear a stammerer on the radio and won't think twice and a whole new generation of real-life superheroes will be laying the path for future generations.

Growing up, I thought I needed a job where I didn't speak because I saw nobody like me anywhere, but change is happening right now!

Of course, how *Love Island* changed the trajectory of my romantic life and career is not to be ignored. It was the biggest change in how I had to think about myself when, suddenly, everyone had an opinion. Whether they'd seen me on the show or not, just hearing I was a *Love Island* contestant gave people a lot of preconceived ideas and judgements. You can lose yourself and your identity in times of upheaval. It helps to know who you are and who you want to be. So much was swirling around me when I came out of the villa, I had to stand still for a second and catch my breath. When a lot of change is happening all at once, even if it *needs* to happen, you owe it to yourself to have regular check-ins. Make sure you can physically and mentally keep up with all the turmoil (both positive and, sometimes, negative) while staying happy and healthy.

My Top Five TV Shows About Change

1. *Gossip Girl* – a major coming-of-age drama about change. You follow each character's

journey from when they were teenagers, through their love stories, leaving school, starting careers, etc.

2. *Ginny & Georgia* - a mum/daughter relationship story about the mum protecting her daughter, but sometimes too much. The show follows how they both handle the daughter changing from child to adult.

3. *Never Have I Ever* - a young girl explores herself and who she is in relation to her heritage, her culture, her friends and her feelings about love, sex and romance.

4. *Blood & Water* - all too easy to binge (I got addicted), this is full of unexpected twists that suck you in and it never gets predictable or dull.

5. *Heartstopper* - the most beautiful show, starring the incredible Bradley Riches, about dealing with mental, physical and societal change. I love watching it. It's about a boy who figures out he's bisexual and falls in love with a friend, and all the implications of that. Ultimately, it's television brilliance about acceptance and being loved.

A change will do you good

Society sometimes labels change as negative, so that when it is forced upon us, we think of it as scary or shameful. Or if we decide to change direction, we're scared others will think us weak, or stupid, or that we can't stick to our goals.

Forget all these preconceived ideas and misconceptions. Because without change, you get stuck. And who cares about what has always been expected of you in the past or for the future – you get to decide. No one knows *you* better than *you*. People can judge, gossip, whatever. But to make changes is brave, sensible and often the only way to move on and move up.

Without risks, we go nowhere. Without taking a gamble, we can't win. Some changes won't pay out. Maybe you'll have to rethink your formula and try a different scheme – but at least you're moving, you're adapting, you're experimenting, you're looking ahead and feeling hopeful that things will improve. Focus on what made you want to make a change in the first place. Do not focus on what others say. And if in doubt, make a list: sort the pros and cons of any changes into two columns. Then read them, multiple times. Think about them. Meditate on them. Do whatever you need to do to see into the future as clearly as any of us can. Engage the heart and the head. Writing it down will really help you see things for what they are.

Making my big move to London meant taking a chance and putting myself out there, especially because I was self-employed. But that's where change can give you another surprising benefit: it can remind you to stay humble, as you start from scratch, meet new people and attempt new challenges that come without guarantees and can be scary, particularly if you are self-conscious about your superpower. Change also keeps you conscientious. You have to work hard to win big, unless you're very, very lucky. The need to pay my rent kept me humble and motivated on my move down to London. And excited – what did the future hold? Change means throwing everything out and dreaming big. You can do it.

Dream Box

In five years' time, I'll look back on all the changes I've made since leaving school and feel so happy I made them. And I want you to be able to do the same. Set yourself this task: right now, write down three dreams - not things like winning an Oscar (unless you're a very talented actor, of course) but dreams that are rooted in your talents, your goals, your hopes - to own a car, to be engaged, to start a degree, to travel to India … Whatever they are, jot them down, date stamp them and file them somewhere safe. Then set a reminder on your phone to check them in one year, five years and ten years. Have you made the changes you needed to make to help those dreams happen? If yes - do you feel grateful, thankful and proud? Good! You should! If no - right, are they still your dreams? If so, what do you need to do differently? Stop wasting time.

Disclaimer on dreams

Sometimes things aren't meant to be. Sometimes our dreams change, along with our circumstances. Sometimes different changes are pushed on you by other people because they're not brave enough to make them on their own. This is when all the lessons we've learned so far in the previous chapters – about loving and respecting yourself, about growing into yourself, about building your resilience – come into play: know your own mind. Is it time to stop trying to make a change that won't ever happen? Are you banging your head against a brick wall? Or are you being brave? If you've given something your best shot, but it's not happening, or doesn't feel right, or your gut is telling you a different direction would be better, make *those* changes instead. You are accountable to yourself, your health and your happiness first.

I've had times in my life when I haven't been sure about things – what I was doing and where I was going, especially when I was a dancer (my all-time career dream) during Covid, when performances were cancelled and, therefore, my contracts were cancelled, too. The impact on my finances was massive (not in a good way), as you can imagine. I was forced to start looking in a different direction for paid work, which was when the idea of modelling came up. Slowly, it started happening for me, my confidence (and bank account) started to bounce back and I thought, *OK, it's not where I thought my career was going, but I can do this*! Dancing will always be my passion – I still take classes when I can, and the dance floor will always be my safe place – but I adapted my dreams and made it work. You can, too.

When change doesn't work out ...

Remember, just because logic or finances or external influences mean you sometimes have to make a change, you don't have to wave goodbye to past loves or past lives for ever. As I said, I still love to dance, and although it may not be my job now, who knows – maybe that helps me to love it even more, as a hobby, which takes the pressure off. And yes, I've left Yorkshire, but I'm still proud to have been born and raised there. You take the memories with you; you take the people (those you want to take) with you. You can have reunions, you can visit, or you can hold up your hands and admit you made a mistake and do a 360-degree turn back to where you came from. Very little in life is set in stone. Don't let the fear of what happens if the change doesn't suit you stop you giving it a go. I'm lucky that I really love what I'm doing now and the big changes I've made have worked out, but I know I won't be stubborn about rewinding or turning back if I ever have to.

The weirdest change: celebrity

Stepping out into the real world from the villa and being well known was a big change and a very odd feeling. Suddenly, I'd find myself on a red carpet or in a room with famous people I'd admired from afar for years and it was very, very surreal. My biggest pinch-me moment was when I landed a brand deal with eBay. I thought, *Can this really be happening?* Then, walking into the National Television Awards to cheering crowds and paparazzi shouting my name, fans asking for photos and autographs, was another moment of craziness. I was just a regular, unknown person before *Love Island*, obviously, but the quick change of status that reality shows can cause should not be underestimated. I hadn't appreciated how big the show was, watched by millions all around the world. We even have fans as far away as Australia. That's a big change!

I know Andrew and I are no longer together but we had one another's backs from day one, understanding when one of us felt overwhelmed, and what could help. The first thing we did when we got out of the villa was book a holiday, just the two of us. That probably sounds strange because in theory we'd just been on a very long holiday – an eight-week one in the villa in the sunshine – but this gave us a week on our own, without gossip or cameras, to slowly accept the changes that were hitting us hard.

I also feel lucky that having already been through a few battles and changes in my life – my deafness, my parents' divorce, the terrible bullying – I stayed grounded, and knew who I was at my core. My ego was in check, my morals, too, and I knew who I could trust.

Today, I might be recognised and get offered exciting projects; in a few years someone else might have taken my place. I have to be OK with all kinds of change and try to keep my feet on the ground. It's amazing to be invited to glam events to do shoots with teams of people making you look fabulous, and getting to talk about things that are important to you. I am having a good time, but I know it probably won't be for ever, and that I need to focus on the changes that will last a lifetime. I'm being sensible with the money I make. I didn't see owning a house in my future at all, even a year ago – it's funny how quickly things change.

It's moments like picking up the keys to a new house when I think, *Gosh – I've worked hard, set goals and I'm reaching them*! Another wow moment was when I started my podcast about people transforming their disabilities and differences into superpowers. That's why I think being born deaf was a gift – because I'm sharing my message to help other people out there break down barriers.

Take a moment

Do your thing. I think it's so important to take breaks, recharge and take some time out on your own to acknowledge that you've been through a lot, you've changed a lot and change is hard. We often focus on the next thing, the next thing and the next thing, always rushing, always changing - and while that is fabulous and brave and worthwhile, it's important to stop, regroup and give yourself a pat on the back sometimes, too. It's not vain or egotistical to reflect on the previous twelve months or whatever and think: *Wow, I did that; that's good.*

The anxiety of change

We've all been there – the night before we start a new job or move to a new town, the morning of our wedding or a long-distance flight to somewhere far, far away – the excitement that mingles with anxious thoughts to give us butterflies in our tummies, bring out the sweats and make sleep or even sitting still impossible. The positivity or excitement and the negativity or anxiety are so interlinked that it can be hard to decipher between the two and get a grip on our emotions, thoughts and fears.

Imagine walking into the villa on *Love Island*, surrounded by strangers, your every screenworthy utterance or inter-action blasted to the public? That was a time when I felt the mingle of both excitement and anxiety, I can tell you! I was aware a lot would change after I went on the show, some of it outside my control. I can still remember vividly making my first entrance, getting dropped off outside the villa doors in a car and the producers telling me to just go in and do my thing – in a bikini. Yes, I was dropped off in a bikini! I was so nervous opening the door, not knowing who'd be behind it, my mind a foggy blur of surrealism, thinking, Am I really here, doing this? Yes, I was scared, there's no other word for it. And I confess I did wonder what on earth I was doing there a few times. But I knew that it was worth the risk. I was doing well modelling at the time, but I knew it wasn't enough for me.

When ITV are recruiting for *Love Island*, you don't always know you've made the cut until close to the start of filming. I didn't even know I'd got through to the final round, but I had a gut feeling (I'd been manifesting being on *Love Island*), so I quit my modelling management team, so they couldn't book me on any jobs, telling a white lie that I was going travelling for the summer – in the hope, of course, that I would be!

When the production team called to say I'd made the final cut, and that I could be away from my life for as long as eleven weeks (if I made it to the final), the anxiety swelled. Isn't the universe crazy? You dream of something, it happens, and then the fear, adrenalin, the risks all pour into your body and brain. You've probably felt it when you've got a promotion you wanted, or a part in a school play, or a date with a person you've fancied for ages – the good and the bad, the excitement and the anxiety can take over. And that's when, as I said earlier, you need to ramp up the grit and guts. Change is a risk, yes, but it will make your life better most of the time. I was excited to go into the villa and put being deaf and how we are treated and accepted out there, via a show watched by people in my peer group.

You're not going to make your life better doing the same thing over and over again. It's like talking to a friend who is dating a terrible person, and having to console them through the same fights, the same complaints, the same tears, when you just want to say to them: stop, reflect, change! You can do it. You wish grit and guts to your friend who is stuck in a bad relationship (or in a job with a bad boss, or in a home that makes them unhappy). Be your own friend, too: wish the same grit and guts to yourself, take a risk and make the change.

A Parent's View

Tasha's mum, Nicky, on finding out about her daughter's hearing loss - and how that changed her parenting journey

Obviously, it was not easy getting the news. Natasha had a couple of tests with a health visitor where they made noises behind her and she was supposed to turn around and she didn't. She then had a brain-stem test which is where we found out she is profoundly deaf. I think by then we knew. The hearing team then stepped in and we met an audiologist in York who helped us and guided us through the steps of what happens next. She was the one at Natasha's appointments doing the hearing checks and measurements for her hearing-aid moulds, and she fitted her first hearing aids and switched them on. I took Natasha to many toddler groups, so she could mix with other children her age, but also took her to a deaf toddler group, too. This was good for me to meet and talk to other mums about their experiences and hear their advice. My family learned sign language along with Natasha, but we also used speech. Natasha was so strong and determined, even at a young age, and that gave me confidence that she would never give in. And she hasn't. As a parent, you obviously want to know why she was born deaf. We had genetic tests, but there was nothing apparent. You think, Have I done something while I was pregnant? We were

> *eventually referred to the cochlear team at Bradford Royal Infirmary and a lady called Jayne visited us on numerous occasions to talk about implants and assess us and Natasha to see if she was a good candidate. She was, and we had an implant date pretty quickly, around her fifth birthday. She then started thriving; there was no stopping her!*

The power of adaptability

It's never too late to change or adapt things that you don't like about your life, or even the things that are just blah and meaningless. You can change your social circle, your career, your purpose, your home, your family relationships ... you can even change your personality, learning to quash the things about yourself that you know are unbecoming or holding you back. Start making the moves that work for you.

- Go for it. Don't second guess yourself.
- It might be scary or daunting but so is being stuck in a rut or stuck with someone who makes you nervous or depressed.
- Trust that once you make that change, you'll feel so much better. You'll look back in time and realise actually you made that change for yourself because you needed it. It could become clear in your relationship, your friendships, etc.

- Change is evolution and revolution for the soul. It makes you grow and expand in directions you may not even be able to imagine right now.

- It may not always work out and that's when you find other paths that you can go down. There are always other journeys you can take. It's about finding your path and eventually life will work out and you'll run at the pace you want to roll. And because you've made one change, or a series of changes, even when they fail, you'll know you are courageous and determined, and the next change won't feel so risky or scary.

- You can always go back to your old ways as well – maybe making a change will make you appreciate how good things were in the first place, be it an old job, partner or hometown. Making a change is a good litmus test for where you will be happiest. Trust the universe. Trust your gut. The grass isn't always greener on the other side.

- Be patient. Hang in there. Life will be hard whether you stay stuck or make a big change, because being a human being is hard. There will be times when you will really struggle, but once you've got through it, you'll look back and say I'm so glad I made that change and I went for it. I am stronger than I ever believed myself to be.

- Empower others to make changes for the better in their own lives, too. Listen to their dreams, act as a mentor or a sounding board, help them make connections and be their cheerleader. Surrounding ourselves with motivated, positive people is a tonic for all of us.

Overthinking: the enemy of change

If we think too much, focusing on all the negatives of change, we might never try anything new – and that would be such a waste of potential for all of us. If you don't listen to your gut and adapt your life with courage, your abilities could be limited, your opportunities reduced. Boldness can be the answer – and knowing yourself and what you are capable of, while ignoring the naysayers and any little voices in your head using words like *no*, or *can't*, or *not good enough*. Action means more than words when it comes to change. Don't sit around lazily analysing and overthinking, boring your friends and family with the same old whining about whatever rut you find yourself in. Yes, you need to engage your brain before making any change: have a solid, sensible look at what is in front of you and what your goals are – as I said previously, make a list, journal, lay out your pros and cons – then move. But don't fester in your inertia, stuck in your own head with thoughts that grind change to a halt. Overthinking only ever leads to underachieving.

I'll give you an example about how I've had to adapt my life to the world around me, and helped people to change, too. I could overthink my deafness, allow my disability to stop me from putting myself forward for things, scared of what people might think of me. Instead of doing that, when I meet a new person, or head into a new work opportunity, I bring it up straight away. Then it's already out the way and I don't have to worry about them finding out, or not want to bring it up in case they offend me. Not many people are educated about deafness or cochlear implants, so instead of overthinking their reaction (or allowing them to overthink mine to theirs), I lay my cards on the table and use our meeting as a chance to let them learn more, ask questions, discuss change in the deaf community and what more can be done. There is no overthinking about how I need to present myself any more. It wasn't always this way, but I've learned to be open and forthcoming. Before *Love Island*, when I used to go on dates with guys, I would say straight away over texts before meeting, 'By the way, I'm deaf and I wear a cochlear implant' and most of the time, the man would be like 'Oh, that's cool', and the matter was dealt with simply and cleanly. It's part of me, I can't change it, and like anything in you that you can't change, you shouldn't worry or stress in your head. All problems are best out in the open. We often catastrophise when we keep things inside our brains.

I got in my head a bit when I was auditioning for *Love Island* because the production company kept making me go for hearing tests, private doctors in private hospitals, so they could assess the extent of my deafness. I couldn't shy away from it – they needed to know – and I couldn't help but wonder how much easier the process was for all the other girls who wanted to go into the villa, but I knew to face it out in the open. Bring it on! My philosophy now is to get it done and get it out of the way (the issues, the fears, the questions . . .). You hear me: get it done and get it out of the way! It's a good way to live. Things always feel bigger, scarier and nastier in your head than when you give them fresh air. I am inundated with messages from people with disabilities who are scared to talk about them, or share their experiences, fearing rejection or ridicule, or just being left out. Stop, I tell them. Get out of your head. The truth is, no one is that focused on you anyway – they're all too worried about what they're up to themselves, doing their own overthinking!

Changes I have yet to make

I want to do more, I want society to change more, to be more accepting of people with disabilities. I'm proud to have been the first deaf contestant on *Love Island*, and also to have been the second deaf contestant on *Strictly Come Dancing*. But we need more. We need real representation, not tokenism. There's so much more to do to empower people with disabilities to feel that they belong, they are deserving, they are equal. That's why I love when I get messages from people who say seemingly small things like, 'I felt brave enough to wear my hair up and show my cochlear implant today at school because you always show yours.' I love that even small changes like that allow people's confidence to grow. I love that when

I post about sign language, or about my headaches, or about being trolled, I'm letting other people in the deaf community know they are not alone, that together we can change the way the world sees us. It will take time, but change is occurring. At high school, I would never have talked about my deafness like I do now. I'd have been embarrassed to mention it. Now, I feel it's part of my mission to share my experiences. This way, as hard as it was at first, I've taught many strangers a thing or two about being kind and understanding to those who are different from them.

Another change I need to think about is my own relationship with my disability as I get older, because things will change. My implant could stop working, or my headaches could get worse. That's why I've never stopped practising British Sign Language, in case that's my only option when I'm older. Technology is changing all the time, so in twenty years what's available to the deaf community could be very different. And as you know by now, I've had my fair share of obstacles and change, which gives me the confidence to know I can handle whatever life throws at me.

Exciting changes are afoot for me too! As I write this book, I'm looking for a new home in or around London. I love interior design, so I'll enjoy going from room to room, making it wonderful and cosy ... making it mine; getting involved in home renovation and interior design for the first time in my life.

Most of the time, you really do get out of life what you put in. With hard work and high hopes, you can make changes work for you. I've done it before and I'll do it again. The next big change I want to make is in my career: I'd love to make a business out of a passion, and start my own clothing brand. I've already got some sketches done, and soon I'll start looking at the manufacturing side of it. I know myself well enough to believe I will get it done. Fashion is my passion. And a change really is as good as a rest.

Embracing You

Five tips for using your social media to highlight the changes in you – how far you've come . . . and where you still need to get to

1. **Be your true self** – the version of you that stands today, after all the changes you've been through. This can be a difficult one (and it's the biggest change I've had to learn when doing social media) – to stop trying to portray something that's not authentic and just be yourself. Be unapologetically you and the right audience will support and love you. Trust me: you can't make everyone happy – you will have trolls, everyone does – but focus on the good followers and the people who support the new, improved you because that's all that matters.

2. **Don't copy others.** Following on from the previous point, if you aren't 100 per cent your

true self, it will shine through, and your audience won't feel connected to you. Yes, you are constantly evolving, but make sure the changes are your own, not borrowed from others. You can take inspiration and ideas – I love seeing what influencers do and how they get their content – but if you copy the way they are, then it's not real for you or your audience. You won't grow and people will be able to see right through it.

3. **Show your changes in a creative way to draw in your audience.** You want to captivate them and keep them engaged. Take them on your journey and they will love to see your growth and feel like they are with you along the way. TikTok is great for short, snappy talking videos – you can really show your personality straight away, and the right people will follow you because of that. You can use Instagram for any kind of content.

4. **You don't have to focus on just one thing.** I love fashion, travel and sharing my superpower. As long as it's positive and real to you, you'll inspire others to change and grow . . . probably more than you'll ever know.

5. **Get nostalgic every now and again.** Flick back to posts from the past and feel pride in how far you've come. And take a minute to think about what you'd still like to change.

chapter six

determination

You've done it before and you can do it now.
See the positive possibilities. Redirect the
substantial energy of your frustration and
turn it into a positive, effective, unstoppable
determination.

Ralph Marston, author

I was born determined. I think I was born with a plan. I had
a vision of what I wanted my life to be like from as long ago
as I can remember, and apart from a few setbacks, I've been
focused on making that plan come true. Believe me, there is
nothing arrogant or presumptuous about this. I knew I'd have
to work hard, be brave, get some grit – and I accepted that. If
you're determined to make your dreams come true – be it to
backpack around Asia, get a degree, become a concert pianist,

throw yourself an unforgettable thirtieth birthday party – you have to accept that challenges will come with that. They might be physical or mental, they might be financial or emotional. It's being determined to overcome the challenges that make those dreams come true. For some reason, the turmoil of my parents' divorce kickstarted my outward determination to do well; that's when my dad in particular noticed my drive to be better. He knew that if I set myself a goal, I'd achieve it. My parents saw that I was not a quitter from a very young age, and when you are born with a superpower that makes you stand out, a difference that you have to learn to grow into and navigate, a determination to succeed is a must-have.

Think about your life now, and what you want to achieve in the next year, or decade. What are you *determined* to do? As we start this chapter, I want to set out a few lessons I've learned about determination:

- Ignore people who tell you that your goal is impossible. Don't allow them to throw you off course. You have that inner gold, remember: determination!
- No dream is too big. If you can dream it, you can be it. Only you know how much you want it and whether you're prepared to put the work in.
- It gets hard. Having an inner drive can be exhausting. The easy option would be to give up. But the easy option isn't necessarily the best one for you. And this is about *you*, remember?

- You can set your own timeframe and adjust it when you need to. Don't be in such a rush for the future that you forget to enjoy where you are. The journey is half the fun.
- Setbacks are a part of life and shouldn't make you feel less determined to carry on. Failure is not only an option, but a great learning tool.
- Many people give up on their goals and dreams halfway through a process – drop out of a course, change their mind about moving to a new city, spend the money they've been saving to put a deposit down on a flat because the end seems so far away. Self-doubt kicks in and it feels easier to fail and admit defeat than to keep going. They don't believe they can do it. I'm here to tell you that your dreams *can* come true. But you have to put in the hard work and keep the faith.

There have been many times when I've found life overwhelmingly difficult, when a little devil on my shoulder has tried to persuade me to take my foot off the pedal, forget about the priorities I've set for myself – give up, basically. Luckily, this stronger voice I was born with was always there to shout over that devil: 'No way, I'm going to keep going, until I've exhausted all the options,' it would say. 'I will get what I strive for and the obstacles I'm facing on the journey will help me appreciate the destination all the more when I get there.' That mentality has got me through so much already and will continue to do so in the future.

MY SUPERHEROES

Tyreece Nye, twenty-four

Be strong. Be true. Be you.

My superpower is my ability to transcend the need for gender norms, to just exist as a person and not the genitalia assigned to me. The way I think, the way I work - people always have an opinion, a lot being negative. But that's not a representation of me, that's a reflection of their character. My word is determination. People will try and break you down. Stop you from growing. Stop you from succeeding and take away your happiness. Don't let them. Be strong. Be true. Be you.

Watch and learn

My dad's determination to build a life for himself and his family has been a key inspiration in my desire to stay focused and reach goals. He came from nothing, but started a business and worked really hard, nurturing it relentlessly, until it became very successful. I watched him go from nothing to something, and I wanted to be like him. That's where I got my inner determination from, probably – seeing him working hard and the hard work paying off. But there was a downside to that, which has also taught me an important lesson: not to become so determined to achieve one particular goal that you lose sight of everything else. My dad let his career take over his life, to the point that he was always working in different countries, and we never saw him because he was never really at home. And that's the thing I said to myself when I embarked on my career: I don't want to be like my dad in that respect. I want to have a balance of still making time to see my friends and family and have some downtime on my own. I still want to be able to enjoy myself and be healthy. Sadly, work took over my dad's life too much. Sometimes that can happen to people, unfortunately. Luckily, it hasn't happened to me yet. I'm determined not to let it. Balance is important, people.

 My Top Five Motivating Movies to Inspire Determination

1. *Dirty Dancing* – a classic! I love how the main character, Baby, works hard and goes for it with her dancing and her heart. She's never danced before, but she's determined to enter the competition.
2. *The Blind Side* – a tearjerker but very inspirational and an amazing story based on reality.

3. *The Devil Wears Prada* - a story about a young woman's career, including horrible bosses and mean colleagues. In the end, she puts herself first, which I love!
4. *Click* - a comedy, but with so much meaning behind it. A workaholic finds a remote control that lets him fast forward and rewind bits of his life, teaching him what is really worth fighting for.
5. *Creed* - a little bit brutal, so not for the faint-hearted, but the way the main character grafts and has real passion for boxing is a lesson in determination for us all.

Cultivating determination

Grit and determination are particularly important when embracing your superpower. You see this in very successful artists, writers and entrepreneurs. It can't be faked, but if you tweak your days a bit, doing more things that keep you motivated and on track, before long you'll have a natural determination to achieve your goals. These are the main things I do to stay determined, to stay on top of my goals and stop myself getting lost in a panic:

- Being passionate is crucial – for whatever it is in life. If you're not passionate about a project, you will give up in the tough times. The first step is to choose something *for you* – not for anyone else. Don't study Italian because your mum wishes she had. It has to be your passion, your goal, if you want an easier ride to the end.

- We all have days where we can't be bothered, and a little slip in determination is fine. Don't beat yourself up over it. Start again tomorrow.

- Use tools to keep you on track. Make a vision board. Write things in your diary that you want to do that day. Meditate on how you want to be, full of drive, ticking things off a to-do list. Keep Notes open on your phone to remember ideas, quotes, etc.

- Ask yourself questions regularly. Perhaps even schedule a goal check-in time every morning, or before bed, or once a month: OK, what's next? What have I achieved today? What shall I focus on next month? Hold yourself accountable.

- Journalling is definitely something I would recommend to anybody. You can write down your feelings, as well as how your day's been. I treat mine like my best friend, sharing things I want to get off my chest and my plans for the future.

- Sometimes when I feel stuck or not motivated, I like to go to the gym or dance around to my favourite music at home. If I hit a block and don't know what to do, getting out of the mental space and into the physical can shake things up in a good way.

Celebrate!

It's important to celebrate your successes so far, as opposed to reminding yourself all the time of what you haven't done. Giving yourself a pat on the back for staying on course will keep you positive about the future. You don't have to throw yourself a party, but maybe you can take the day off and do something you love, or take an extra-long, hot shower and reflect on all the big ticks you've achieved so far. Whatever it is, live in the moment a little to celebrate your achievements. I would suggest also saying things to yourself out loud – 'I'm proud that I did this.' Praising yourself in this way is a really, really good affirmation, putting it out there to the universe. It also acts as a wake-up call of appreciation of what you've done for yourself.

What drives you?

Working out what drives you (but not your partner or your parents or strangers on social media) is crucial to staying de-termined in life. And don't be embarrassed or feel guilty by what motivates you; for example, some people can be driven by ambition and money – you do you! Sit down and really think about your goals, and how you hope to feel or be seen when you've achieved them. Is it all about building your self-worth? Or being appreciated by your peers, or respected by your family? The more self-awareness you have around why you're doing what you're doing, the easier it will be to stay driven.

I would say happiness is what drives me onwards. I don't care about money. I don't care about fame. I don't really care what other people think about me. But I do care about being happy and helping those I love to feel happy, too. If I don't have joy, what is the point of chasing my dreams? I might be rich, respected and famous, but if I'm depressed, lonely or sad, what's the point? Success, to me, is being able to do what I love and make a difference, without sacrificing time with my friends and family.

Purpose power

A sense of purpose is very important. We might think having a fancy car or big house is what gets us out of bed in the morning, but actually, it's waking up and wanting to achieve something with our day, with our lives, that gives everything true meaning.

Having a sense of purpose makes me happy and keeps me motivated. Absolutely. And my purpose is to give a voice and a face to the deaf community, and to give those people confidence and recognition. After doing *Love Island*, I said to my management team that the deals with L'Oreal Paris, eBay, Ann Summers and Sky are all brilliant, and I'm grateful. I pinch myself all the time and I don't get too carried away. It is my purpose within the deaf community that keeps me grounded, keeps me driven to succeed and makes me happy. That's why it's been important to me to always make the time to work with charities, talk about my disability in interviews and share content on my social media about my life as a deaf woman. Deaf people in the public eye are still very few and far between, and role models and advocates can really help (I know I'd have loved to have seen more deaf people on television when I was growing up), which is why I will keep reaching out in all ways open to me, to share my story and listen to those with disabilities. The more we do that, the more we become powerful – and the more we feel confident enough to own our superpowers. Working not just for myself but for my community drives me forward and keeps me in line. I'm not just here for me; I'm here to represent all deaf people. That is my purpose. What is yours?

Take a few minutes to zoom out on your own particular goal or dream, and see if you have a wider purpose, too? Do you want to help your family, your school, your town? Working out a wider purpose can often help to boost your determination to succeed.

A Parent's View

Tasha's mum, Nicky, on staying determined for herself and her child

Our optimism and determination that Tasha would lead as normal a life as possible came from the support we had from the hearing team of experts around us, but mostly from Tasha herself. From the moment she had hearing aids, just before she was one year old, she never took them out. She enjoyed learning and loved music. She didn't let her disability stop her from doing things and we encouraged her to do what she wanted to do. I never classed – or class – myself as having a disabled daughter; she is just my daughter, like any other daughter.

Being driven by the right things

Are you pushing towards your goals for the right reasons?

It's important to be driven but it's also important to be happy and feel a sense of purpose. For example, money is a driver that needs to be balanced with other things, too, I think. I do believe it can buy you happiness, but only in the short term. You can have money one day, but it might be gone the next. And you can't rely on money like you can your friends and family, or your own inner sense of purpose. Because of my distrust of money, I've always been more of a big saver than a splashy spender. I think about my future. I think about what I'll have in twenty years and what I'll need in forty years. I'm strict with what I spend, checking what comes out and what goes in. I want to have as much saved in the bank as I can when I have children and ten more dogs. My future dream life is going to be expensive ... and full of cuteness!

Both money and fame can attract the wrong people into your world. If you achieve sudden riches or celebrity, make sure you have the right people around you. People who knew you before the outward signs of success came your way. They are the ones to hold on to, cherish and share your life with. Or maybe find people who have been through a similar journey to you and understand where you are currently – supporters, not the ones who were never there for you or even made the effort with you. Remember, trust your gut and look for the genuine in all things.

I wouldn't say I'm famous, but I am in the public eye, and I'm going to let you into a secret: it can have many positives, but it can also have its downsides. Once you're in the public eye, everyone has an opinion about you, and many people want you to fail. There's a pressure on you every time you leave the house that you might get photographed, and you miss the anonymity of your life pre-celebrity. I can't even imagine what fame must feel like at a Kardashian level. Unbearable at times, I'm sure. I would not want to deal with what they have to deal with. Would you? To have every look, relationship, comment scrutinised and picked apart, looking for the negative. Think about that before you blindly pursue celebrity.

Sometimes I wonder what it would be like if no one batted an eyelid when I went into Tesco, would I be relieved? I'm not worried about losing the attention because I'm happy in my life.

I'm excited about the future. I now have a really good fan base outside viewers of *Love Island*. My fan base is people with disabilities, mostly women, and we support each other. I don't rely on them to feed my ego; we rely on each other to lift us all up together.

At the end of the day, *you* know *you*. Be honest with yourself when you set your goals. Dig deep and work out what would make you happy – or happier. The thing you should be most determined about is getting to a place where you know and love yourself. It might sound cheesy, but it's true. You have to be focused on yourself and the biggest thing I've learned is not to rely on other people's opinions. It's not a bad thing if fame is something you dream of, go for it, but go into it knowing who you are and your purpose.

My future goals

I haven't achieved everything I want to – not by a long shot. I think it's a good thing to look forward, update your dreams and expect more of yourself. Sure, we need to live in the moment, but always with an eye to what is next if we have the energy to keep going.

Obviously one of my biggest dreams came true when I was chosen for *Strictly Come Dancing*. I felt like Sam Thompson when he went into the jungle in *I'm A Celebrity . . . Get Me Out of Here!* I felt grateful for every new routine and humbled by the different people I got to work with on something entertaining and special. I loved watching Sam open up to a wider audience about his ADHD, being in his element as his most authentic self. You could tell at moments he couldn't believe he was there, and his genuine heart leapt off the screen. That is when fame is a good thing: it allows you to do things you otherwise wouldn't be able to do – like going into the jungle or dancing with professionals every week live on the BBC – and it allows you to share your trials and tribulations with people who might need to know they are not alone.

The trials of reality TV

I went through a lot on *Love Island* – it's unnatural to be trapped with strangers with no outside contact for so long. Viewers probably imagine we're all just chilling, on holiday in the sun, but that's not how it works. There are tasks to do and inevitably not everyone is going to get on, so there are days when there is tension in the air or people having arguments.

I'm a very sensitive person, so I spent quite a lot of the show crying because that's how I express my emotions, and once I'm set off, I can't stop the tears. The crying made people dislike me even more, and I was getting torn apart by the outside world. I was really tough on myself for that because I felt like I was letting down the deaf community. I'd think to myself, *What am I doing; why am I hated so much?*

Before I left, my dad had given me a bracelet, telling me to wear it on screen if I wasn't doing well, to let him know when I wasn't in a good place. And I did wear it once after a rough day. But I got an attitude adjustment from that moment, and the last four weeks of filming were the most amazing experience for me – when I was truly happy, truly myself and Andrew and I decided to properly get to know each other – so I don't want to look back and turn the end of my time on the show into a negative. We stopped caring about what the other contestants thought and just enjoyed ourselves. Once we'd left the show, I moved past it as much as I could, as quickly as I could. I didn't even watch my series when I got out – not a single episode. Maybe when I'm forty, I'll be ready to sit down and watch it.

Being unapologetically yourself

I was determined to be unapologetically myself during the last few weeks of *Love Island*, as an individual and as one half of a couple. I realised that not everyone will like you or be on your side, so the most important thing is to like *yourself* and be on your *own* side. And that's what I'd say to people now, especially those with disabilities or differences: embrace who you are, and the right people will understand and appreciate you. Don't be ashamed of anything, and be real with those who deserve your time, attention and affection.

Where I've gone wrong in the past is caring too much about what people thought about me. I lost myself because I was trying to live up to their expectations, trying to change how I was and what I was trying to be. Then I realised what a waste of time that was. I thought, *What am I doing? This is not who I am.* The best advice I can give you is to be who you are and not think about outside opinions, because if you let them get to you, that's when you lose your best, strongest, most beautiful self. Instead of striving towards your goals with determination, you'll waste time second guessing yourself, worrying about what others think. Obviously, if someone I trust and respect is giving me feedback, I'll listen, but criticism from someone I don't admire? No thanks. That's their opinion, and I don't need it. In the villa, when Andrew and I stopped caring and started being who we wanted to be as a couple, we thrived. We were happy, focused on ourselves and each other.

How to accept that you are enough

- You just have to believe in yourself. And you have to trust in yourself as well. You are your own best bet.

- Comparison is the thief of joy. Look inwards instead of outwards when deciding what you want to do, where you want to go and who you want to be. Don't look for all the answers on social media. We are all unique and that's what makes us special.
- The right people will love you, the wrong people might not. I've learned in this career, and in life in general, that not everyone's going to love and understand me and that's OK. You can't make everyone love you. Focus on the ones who do.
- Be appreciative of those who allow you to be your authentic self because they are the ones who will get you through the tough times. You need to determinedly keep them around you. There's a saying: the people who matter don't mind and the people who mind don't matter. I love that because it's so true. We can try and fit in, or we can try and change ourselves to make people like us, and some people will never like us because we remind them of an ex-partner, or they don't like tall people, or something irrelevant to you. People come at you with all their own prejudices and their history, and you can't change it. You just have to be you because everyone else is taken. Be authentically, unapologetically you!

Embracing You

Five things to cultivate the determination and motivation to make your way in the world

These are things that help me stay determined and motivated as I make my way through life's daily trials and tribulations.

1. **Going to a dance class.** Let loose and get lost in music. It's a time when you can be who you want to be, put on a character and go for it! No one judges you in this supportive space.

2. **Take care of yourself.** Go get your nails done, have a massage or go to the salon for a blow-dry. These little things can really boost your self-confidence, the external improvements boosting internal emotions. For example, I didn't feel that confident with my short hair, so I got long extensions in and now I feel fabulous!

3. **Be your own cheerleader.** Always be proud of yourself. Do you ever sit down quietly and look back, reminisce and be proud of what you've done? Remembering how far you've come will assure you that you will be OK – you've done it before, and you can do it again!

4. **Get out of your comfort zone.** Take risks and you will grow in confidence, regardless of whether they go smoothly or not. Either way,

you'll have pushed yourself and grown as a
person.

5. **Look in the mirror and say three positive
    things about yourself.** Out loud. Think of the
    things you love about yourself and tell them to
    your reflection. I try to do this every morning, so
    I feel great in myself for the rest of the day.

chapter seven

learning

There are no regrets in life, just lessons.

Jennifer Aniston

Life is one big lesson – doesn't it feel that way a lot of the time? When friendships or relationships fail, flourish or change, we learn about ourselves, how we think, how we share, what brings us peace and happiness and, perhaps most importantly, what we want for ourselves in the future. When we start a new job or a new class at college, we learn about social constructs, how to be brave and what we want from life. My most meaningful lesson, throughout my life, has been how to handle my disability, and how to share it with the world in a positive way. I will never stop learning from other people I meet in the deaf community, or about what my interactions can do for those around me.

We all take lessons with us every day, the good, bad and ugly, each of them helping to harness the superpowers we've talked about so far (how to love, grow, change, how to build our self-respect, resilience and determination), along with our sense of responsibility (in the next chapter). Only a fool would think he knows it all and has nothing else to learn. In fact, the more I know, the more I realise I *don't* know. Make it your mission to keep looking for the lessons by reading more, listening more, travelling more, sharing stories and being open to new experiences.

What I can teach

Representing people with hearing loss or deafness is the most important thing to me. And taking a stand for people with any disability and opening people's eyes to how we function in the world – a world we all deserve to be equally a part of. I know that's my biggest superpower. If you're feeling different or alone, with a quirk or disadvantage that makes you feel less than, stop. Don't feel embarrassed or ashamed. We need to be out there, making things happen, and we deserve to be on television, to be seen and heard, to be accepted. I never had that when I was growing up. I never had someone who I could watch or read about who made me feel comfortable, understood and represented.

Times are changing, thankfully, and things are getting better for those of us with disabilities, but there's still a lot of work to be done in educating people, and you can play an important role in making that happen. You can help by teaching those around you how it feels to be you and how they can welcome you. We need to be in all media, and in every industry, accepted for what makes us different, rather than being shunned for it. This lack of representation is what drove me to go on *Love Island*. I thought, *This is a moment where I can really show my generation what it means to be different; I can teach them to be kind.*

There have been deaf women on *The Great British Bake Off* and *Strictly Come Dancing* now, too, but we don't need to stop there. It's not a case of, 'Oh, we can tick that box now. Deaf woman – done!' Television producers wouldn't say, 'We've had one blonde; that's enough blondes' or, 'We've had a very tall man on the show, let's not feature any more tall men for a while.' People with disabilities should be constantly and consistently featured in our media, not as a one-off to fill a quota of inclusivity. Our society will be so much stronger when we normalise the things that were previously pushed into the shadows. The quicker we learn that we are all different, but all valuable, the better. I want to be one of those voices for the younger generation and guide them as much as I can. Without representation, people can feel isolated and lost. Let's stop that.

My Top Five Books for Lessons in Love and Self-love

These books have taught me valuable life lessons. And one of them has allowed me to escape into a new world, too. I couldn't be the person I am today without these great reads on my bookshelf – from strong female characters to self-help.

1. *The Power of Letting Go: How to Drop Everything That's Holding You Back* by John Purkis.

2. *Men Are from Mars, Women Are from Venus: A Practical Guide for Improving Communication and Getting What You Want in Your Relationships* by John Gray.

3. *A Gentle Reminder* by Bianca Sparacino.

4. *The Mind Manual: Mental Fitness Tools for Everyone* by Dr Alex George.
   And last, but not least …

5. The *Bridgerton* series by Julia Quinn (always good to unwind with).

Sharing is caring

A huge part of learning comes from getting feedback from those we trust, and those experiencing similar things. What could we do better, differently or promote more of? Through various channels, I get a lot of feedback from people who have a disability themselves, or whose child or sibling or friend has a disability. When I first came out of the villa, I didn't realise what an impact I'd made – my mum and dad had to tell me. And when I started looking through my messages, which were 80 per cent to do with disabilities, thanking me ('You made me feel understood . . . Now I feel like I can talk to my friends about what is going on with me'), I was thrilled. That's all I ever wanted to do; my passion is to help those people gain confidence.

I learn from the anecdotes my followers share. There's one mother and her daughter, who also has a cochlear implant, and we've stayed in touch ever since the show, the mum keeping me updated about her daughter's check-ups and how she's feeling. Every story I hear furthers my faith in what humans can do and how much we help each other. And it's made me realise that how I use my voice is important.

You don't have to be famous to lend a voice to your community; you can be an advocate to one person or a million. Before *Love Island*, I had a small presence on Instagram, about 10,000 followers. I started something very small called *Talks with Tasha*, sharing inspirational quotes and thoughts I'd had about my disability. The people who needed it found it and loved it, and that inspired me to keep going and do more. We can always do more of the things that we're good at. Speak to charities, set up a themed Facebook group. Find out what works for you in the community you want to be a part of. Research your topic, find a mentor, learn about the space you're in and what is missing.

A Parent's View

Tasha's mum, Nicky, on the lessons she's watched her daughter learn

I am so very proud of Natasha. Not just because of Love Island and what she has done since but how she has been throughout her journey so far. Nothing stops her doing what she wants to do; she will always find a way to do it. She has a superpower and she is using it to promote and highlight inclusivity and inspire others. We have had so many messages from parents of deaf children who had no confidence to show their cochlear implants, saying that Natasha has given them hope and that their children are now proud to show their implants. One lady had a baby only a few months old and she now has two implants. She didn't know about implants before she saw Tash on Love Island. Natasha has given these parents and children a role model. I am a very proud mum and love her for being herself.

Learning about difference

I would say to you, reader, that if someone in your life has got a disability, go and do your research to find out what they're going through and how you can make their life better. There's so much on YouTube and TikTok on every topic. Or just google it or go to the library. Do what you need to, so that you have that foundation of understanding. And if the person in question is comfortable enough to talk about it, ask them questions. Look at the world from their point of view. Find out what works for them and what doesn't. For me, I find it wonderful when people learn British Sign Language. When my friends and family learned it, I felt included and not left out any more. There are always little things you can do that will make someone feel less isolated.

Learn to be patient with a friend or family member with a disability, or with something happening in their life that is causing trauma or upset. Patience is so important. They might not want to talk yet; but one day, you listening to them with an open mind and heart could be the most healing thing in the world for them. You won't be able to fully understand what they're going through but supporting them with love and compassion will mean the world. I know. I've been that outsider who was so grateful when people reached out to me. And if they're having tough times, just be with them. Be there with a kind word, or a hug or a packet of biscuits. Be there quietly, so they know they are not alone. I'm grateful to my parents for being there in those moments when I was sullen or angry, confused and upset. It was hard to stay there, by my side, while I spouted hatred at them, but they did, and it made an immeasurable difference to how I am today.

Lessons I've Learned the Hard Way

'My Pain, My Mistake, My Lesson' - this is a good, practical exercise you can do to think about what a difficulty or a dilemma has taught you, and what you'd do differently in the future. Grab a pen and paper, read my example (below), then think about some from your own life.

My pain ...
I really let my superpower of being deaf define me, so much so that it was beating me down. It affected my mental health to the point where I would lock myself in the bathroom and cry for hours. I would ask myself, why me? Why not someone else? Especially as a teenager - that's when it hit me the most. I would compare myself to others and worry that I had no career and love life ahead of me. I was so concerned about people's judgements, thinking that they were always secretly talking about my cochlear implant.

My mistake …

I wanted to blame someone, to lash out, so I decided to blame my parents for making me deaf. I was in so much pain, I used to inflict my pain on them. I would throw my cochlear implant to the point of breaking it. I really utilised my anger in the worst way possible, bottling it all up and then, eventually, I'd explode. I would shout at them; I would cry in frustration. What I didn't know back then is that most people don't care about you or how you look; they only care about themselves! My mistake is that I wasted so much time worrying about others' opinions when really, they had their own things to be worrying about.

My lesson …

I've learned that actually my disability is a gift, and I regret blaming it on my parents so much. I'm so thankful for them and I love them with all my heart. It has been a massive lesson in my life that sometimes we can't change a situation; we can only control what we can and try to adapt to what we can't. Being born deaf was something my parents couldn't control. They are my superheroes and I'll always be grateful that they were so patient with me. Being deaf isn't a negative, I can see that now. Being deaf has made me grow as a person and helped me to form a hard shell to make me strong. Allow your superpower, or powers, to make you strong, too. I know already that you are!

chapter eight

responsibility

A year from now you may wish you had
started today.

Karen Lamb, author

Whatever road you are on, however much you want to get
to your dream destination, a million distractions will pop
up and try to sway you from going in the best direction.
Even when you know a move, a job, a relationship – whatever it is – needs your focus and energy, there will be
pushes and pulls from other areas, glittery objects vying
for your attention, and people who, consciously or not, will
be trying to lure you off your path, away from your goals
and living your happiest, healthiest life. And this is where
it ends, with you: don't get distracted; take responsibility
for yourself and your actions. They're your dreams, your

goals. You and you alone are responsible for making them come true.

I feel like, as a society, we're finding it increasingly hard to take the blame, say sorry, hold our hands up and own our shit. The bad news is – we have to, if we want to grow as people, as partners and professionals. And this chapter will, I hope, help you to do that. Are you ready to be held accountable? Ready to use your superpower for the wider good? I'd argue you have a responsibility to let your differences shine. So let's go.

My take on responsibility

I'm not someone who gets distracted very often. I'm quite good at keeping myself on my toes and doing what I need to do. That wasn't always the case, of course. A few years ago, I'd go out and party too much and drink too much, and not only would that consume a lot of my time at night, but the next day I'd feel less than my best and unable to do much other than sleep off a hangover slumped on the sofa. We all need those days of being sociable, of course, but not to the detriment of every other aspect of our lives. Once I realised what an overactive social life was taking from other parts of my world, I cut out the stuff I didn't really want to do, got more discerning about what I put on my calendar and found that my determination and conscientiousness returned. I can work much harder when I'm keeping my drinking and late nights in check. Are you the same?

And I want to work hard, to push myself, because I do have (and have had, ever since I was a teenager, according to my parents) an innate sense of responsibility for how my superpower is accepted in society, and for the deaf community to be seen and heard and to be given the same freedoms as everyone else.

Sometimes this responsibility can feel like a burden. It can make me feel tired and rundown, and then I know I need to step away from my crusade and just Netflix and chill for the afternoon or for the weekend. We all need a break sometimes, a healthy distraction from the outside world, but we have to decipher between a genuine rest and being lazy. I'm getting better at putting work aside sometimes, but with everything on the phone, and the phone always in our hands, it's hard to switch off completely. We must, though! We must train ourselves to leave our phones elsewhere and engage properly with a film or a show or in a conversation with a friend when we need to unwind from the weight of the world.

Other times, this responsibility that I feel to make the world a better, easier place for people with my (or any) superpower feels like a gift – it's a true passion that keeps me motivated, inspired, active and hungry for more. I'm sure yours motivates you to keep going onwards and upwards, too, doesn't it? As I said in the Introduction, and I truly believe: sometimes a sense of responsibility to change something, to do something, can feel like a mountain you have to climb. Every. Single. Day. But do keep going – you owe it to yourself and to others. And the view from the top will be worth it.

MY SUPERHEROES

Cambell Kenneford, twenty-nine

Trans people are the same as everyone else

I'm a full-time content creator, and my content is based around my transition and making it feel light-hearted, to show that trans people are the same as everyone else. I feel that this is my superpower: being able to spread my message and educate people on the issues that trans and LGBTQ+ people face. I use this in every aspect of my life, and this is my uniqueness that I can offer the world. I never used to embrace my differences and would shy away from being different, but now I use that superpower to make a change and be my brightest and sparkliest self.

Only you can make *you* happy

Yes, of course, friends and family may fill your world with joy and fun, but, ultimately, you're responsible for your own happiness. I've always been quite independent; someone who'll say, 'Right if I want this to happen, I need to make it happen. I'm not gonna beg my mum or dad for it. I'm not gonna rely on other people. I'm gonna put the hard work in.' Learning about the responsibility I hold within myself, *for* myself, was quite a big thing for me. I've always been very independent. I've always been the girl who likes me-time, enjoying my own company, chilling out in my bedroom, and I think that's crucial: working out how to be content on your own, not reliant on other people for entertainment. Now, in my twenties, I'm that person who can sit on their own in a café or restaurant and enjoy a meal, oblivious to those around me, not worried about looking like I have no friends. If I want to see a certain show or eat a particular thing, being alone isn't a hindrance to that. I'll do what I want to do, and if others are around great, but if they're not, I'll do it anyway.

If you're someone who feels awkward being out and about on your own, remember this: no one else is looking at you or cares what you're up to. They're all too busy worrying about themselves. Appreciating this is liberating, even if you might be more self-conscious than most because of your superpower. Be free, have fun. Don't wait for others to agree to meet you. This even goes for holidays. Some people love travelling on their own, on their own schedule. Truly, being happy in your own company is a wonderful ability to have.

And it's so important to have time to yourself – to unwind, to plan, to focus on your own self-care and to build your confidence. Obviously, when I was single, I was a much more independent person because when you are on your own, you have to figure out what to do with yourself. But I still value alone time now. I'm very good at not relying on other people to fill my social calendar or self-love bank. Do you do things just for you? Are you making time to work on what makes you happy, even if no one else wants to join you? It might be hard to persuade people to go to a gym class or start volunteering at a food bank with you, but that shouldn't stop you doing it. You really are responsible for your own happiness and sense of purpose.

My Top Five Tunes to Help You Own Your Shit

I put these songs on loud when I want to dig into my emotions, build up my confidence and shake off any negativity. Whenever I hear this music, I feel capable of taking responsibility for my own life and making it better.

1. 'Cannonball' by Little Mix – makes me feel alive. The lyrics especially are so relatable.
2. 'Proud' by JLS – this makes me feel that I hope I've made my parents proud. Everything I do in life is for them, and when I hear this song, it brings back childhood memories of when I was little, dreaming big, and here I am making them proud.

3. 'Hey Brother' by Avicii - just a great, whole-some song! It's upbeat and I love to turn the volume up when I hear it. It reminds me of my brother, Alex, who lives in Australia. I rarely get to see him, and when we connect it's very special. So this song is about Alex for me.

4. 'Aeroplanes' by B.o.B. - an iconic one! It's a dreamy song that makes me feel like any-thing is possible.

5. 'My Universe' by Coldplay - all about love and who you really care about.

Get organised

You have probably guessed by now that I am a very organised person. Without a good system around my calendar and to-do list, I'd crumble. It's important to take responsibility for what is expected of you, and where and when – anything less is stressful! It's a much calmer and easier way to live when you've planned out what you need to do and when. I couldn't cope with the mental chaos of not knowing where I have to be or what I need for a work event or a meeting or even what to pack for a holiday. Seriously, being organised is a superpower. Maybe the most undervalued one, because it's not very sexy, is it, being a planner? But it is a true superpower that can give you back your sanity and save you time and stress.

My big planning day is Sunday, when I look through my diary and see what I have on for the next six days. Then I look forward even further, maybe even to a trip I'm taking two months in the future and note down what I need to buy or pack. I plan my outfits for any events I have coming up, make sure they're clean, wrinkle-free and ready to wear. I like to be ahead of the game. I hate being stressed out at the last minute, and my Sunday planning sessions help me avoid any rising panic and allow me to feel so much more content and calm, limiting any nasty surprises.

Professionally, I use a spreadsheet to mark down what needs to be done – what content I've shot for my social media, what's been approved, what needs to be edited. That way, I'm always on track and know what I need to do and how to use the time I have. We always think we'll remember what we have to do, but we don't. There's a lot of stuff flying around our brains at any given time and it really helps to just write it down. When I know my work spreadsheet is up to date, I can relax on the sofa or go to the gym with a clear head. I also add all work meetings and events into my phone calendar the minute they are confirmed, and schedule in getting-ready and travel time around them, blocking that out, too. This, in turn, allows me to plan for my social life, too: I know when I'll be free for fun and can put seeing friends in the diary accordingly. Honestly, keeping your calendar and to-do list up to date is one of the best things you can do for yourself. You'll feel so much calmer when your ducks are all in a row. I find I even sleep better, too. So don't rely on other people to remind you where you have to be or what you should be doing. That's an anxiety-inducing way to go through life. Take responsibility instead – and put yourself in control.

A Parent's View

Tasha's dad, Tarek, on teaching his daughter what he considers to be one of life's most important values: responsibility

Naturally, children learn values from their parents, and Tasha learned about responsibility observing the actions of us both: me and her mum. She and her brother, Alex, were responsible for keeping their bedrooms tidy (although they rarely were) and they were given age-appropriate chores to earn rewards they valued, such as going bowling or to Frankie & Benny's for dinner. And Tasha was in charge of feeding our pet cat and rabbit.

Responsibility, in terms of owning bad behaviour and digesting why it was not acceptable, was not so easy to convey with only sign language at our disposal when Tasha was younger, but we did our best to help her understand that it was hurtful, and she responded to that. She didn't like or agree with being told off or being made aware of any wrongdoing in her teen years, though. Perhaps this was a normal puberty issue, coupled with frustration in coming to terms with deafness and our unsettled family environment (she spent half the week with me and half with Nicky). We kept talking, though, and now she is a glowing example of how to own something she has done and take responsibility for her actions, even if it still takes her a day or two to process it.

I tried my best to instil financial responsibility in her from a young age, too, in particular how important it is to work for your money and only buy what you can afford, but again, in her teens, Tasha didn't want to work. She would find excuse after excuse, and I soon realised it was a confidence issue, rather than her being lazy. For example, the idea of waitressing and getting someone's order wrong because she did not hear it correctly worried her greatly. Eventually, she got an appropriate job at a garden centre and a light bulb switched on as she learned how empowering it is to earn your own money.

Owning your shit

If you make a mistake, you need to own it, as soon as you can. That can be hard to do, and sometimes it still takes me a bit of time, as my dad has helpfully pointed out above – thanks, Dad! If I know I've messed up, or know I can do better, I can now accept that and apologise to whoever I may have let down. It's not easy, but it's the only way to move forward. I would say it took me a while to own my shit, but I'm at the point now where I know it's the best way.

If I have a strong view that is different to that of others around me, I've learned to back it up and I own that, too. I deliver my opinions fairly and kindly, at the right time and place to the right people, and always listen to what others have to say. And if I'm wrong or misinformed, I'll own it. My main thought is always: *I own my shit, you own yours.* I don't want to get into fights or disagreements with people, and I'm always prepared to learn. I've also learned that when people ask you for your opinion, sometimes they genuinely want to hear it, but more often than not, they're spoiling for a fight and can't be swayed. In those situations, I stay neutral with an attitude of you do you – whatever makes you happy. I am strong within myself in what I feel is true and right, but I don't need to convert people through force. I'd rather educate them with facts and examples.

Saying sorry is still tricky for me, though (ask my brother!), but I am getting better at it. I've learned that even if the blame is equally shared, saying sorry is the best stepping stone towards making amends. It finally clicked with me that apologising isn't a sign of weakness – it's the opposite. It's normally the bigger person who comes forward with an olive branch, wanting to clear up tension or an unresolved dilemma. And I want to be a bigger person. I always try to be that person because I don't want to go to bed in a bad place. I don't need that negativity. I'm realising that a heartfelt, honest apology is one of the most powerful tools in any relationship.

Signs that you can own your shit

1. You can see the bigger picture and understand other people's perspectives.
2. You can laugh at yourself.
3. You're not easily offended, knowing that most people have good intentions.
4. You hold your ground without being rude or aggressive.
5. You know you're not perfect and are always looking for ways to improve yourself.

How to accept your limits

I've discovered that it's actually healthy for me to know my weaknesses, to work on them, to learn from them and not be ashamed of them – especially anything I feel is linked to my superpower. Everyone has weaknesses. We can't all be good at everything. But knowing what they are – perhaps timekeeping, exercise, eating well – also gives you the chance to work on them, if you really do want (or need) to improve in those areas.

We can be responsible for positive change with hard work. For example, I know I'm naturally good at creating content for my social media platforms and putting looks together when I go out or to share on my Instagram, whereas it doesn't come naturally to me to be super punctual. But I'm always on time and very efficient, especially when it comes to posting and work, because I don't like to let people down. Even on the days I do shoots or go to events, I will literally be editing my content on the way or when I get home ASAP. It comes from dancing – we're taught to be professional, we're taught to have discipline. We can all take responsibility for upping our game. If I suddenly decided I wanted to be an opera singer . . . Well, I'd have to accept my limitations there. It's not going to happen. But if the only limits on my possibilities are caused by me being late and being lazy? Self-awareness will allow me to change and improve those negative limitations.

And you can, too. Recognise whether your limits are set in stone, or if they can be pushed with a little grit, grind and self-responsibility. It's about knowing your values and that, actually, it's OK to have limits – everyone's got to. Accepting them will stop you crumbling with self-defeat and exhaustion. And you should also willingly accept limits when it comes to your time and energy. You can't do it all. I limit myself to two jobs a day for example, however tempting it might be to say yes to three or more. I know that mentally, physically and logistically, more than two will be difficult for me. I set limits when I go out socially, too. It's fun to be out for a few hours, but if I'm out for longer than that I risk getting a headache. After three hours, I'll escape the social chaos to get back to my place. I'll nestle in, happy I made the effort and had some fun, but glad I know my limits, content to be home.

My sense of responsibility has strengthened with age. Ultimately, we are all responsible for setting limits on our lives: our time, energy, expectations. Others may want to take more from you, more than is fair or healthy: stand up for yourself and only give what you can give. You may want to do something more (your own worst enemy, on occasion), but be self-aware enough to focus on what you can sustain. Overstepping a personal limit is not good in the long term. Don't be scared to say no, to others and to your worst self. Women in particular feel they should say yes to everything. We don't have to. Sometimes we get FOMO and worry about missing out on work or fun. Again, self-awareness is key here: listen to your gut, listen to your body. Responsibility is a superpower we can all acquire with practice – a superpower that will make us bolder, stronger and wiser.

Embracing You

Five ways to improve your sense of responsibility

How can you make a difference? Is it worth even trying to? Yes, you can and YES!!! Making a difference feels good, makes the endorphins flow, boosts your mood ... and you have a responsibility to yourself and your community to try. Here are some good methods to help you give back:

1. **If you are interested in social media, utilise it for positivity.** There are so many ways you can do this; you can set up a motivational page where you share your experiences and story through quotes

or selfie talking videos. Engaging content really brings in the right audience who will support you. It's the most amazing feeling knowing you have people following you because they believe in you, no matter how few or many. Changing or motivating *one* person is better than none.

2. **Podcasting is a great way to make a difference.** Podcasts are so popular nowadays, and so accessible. It's really effective for sharing your message and you can make it an authentic reflection of yourself. It can be funny, it can be personal and you can have guests on your podcast, too.

3. **Think about learning basic British Sign Language.** This is my personal crusade and you can help: if you have anyone in your family, school or at work who is deaf, or is among one of the many other people out there who use British Sign Language, it really goes a long way to making them feel accepted and loved. And you'll feel great knowing that you've made that person feel included.

4. **Challenge yourself for charity**. I love to raise awareness and do challenges for charity. If you enjoy a run, for example, challenge yourself for the London marathon to raise money for a charity close to your heart. It's so important to give back, and even if you can make a difference

for just one person, that's incredible, and a worthy
responsibility to take on.

5. **Be responsible for your impact on someone
    else's day.** Play your part in the smooth running
    of society, be it not pushing in in a queue,
    giving way in traffic, saying thank you. Being
    responsible for putting a smile on someone else's
    face will make you feel amazing.

my new superpower

While writing this book I discovered a new superpower that I didn't know I had – and that's learning how to pick yourself up after heartbreak. Andrew and I decided to break up after two and half years together and it was a really emotional time for us both.

I guess the cracks started to appear when we were no longer spending as much time together as we usually would – and this made us realise we wanted different things in life. I was appearing on *Strictly Come Dancing* and was lucky enough to make it to the finals. That meant thirteen weeks of training, then rehearsals, and the live shows every Saturday. It was a dream for me to make it to the end – to be in the final with Chris McCausland, JB Gill and Sarah Hadland was just magical. I loved every moment of my

Strictly experience and it's truly one of the best things I have ever done.

Andrew supported me during this time, visiting me in rehearsals and coming to a few live shows. But the more time we spent apart, the more I realised our relationship had run its course and that we had been growing apart. We ended up having a really candid conversation about our future together. It wasn't something either of us saw coming and no one else was involved. The truth is, we were simply destined for different directions. It was a really tough decision.

I didn't want to hurt Andrew, but I knew deep down in my heart that it wasn't right to continue. There were a lot of tears and it was a really hard time because neither of us truly thought this time would come. Andrew was, at one point, the man I was going to marry. We had discussed having children in the future and we had bought a house together. We also had our little dog, Luna.

We were in it for the long haul, but I felt that something had changed between us. I started to feel differently about the future and felt that we were no longer on the same page. As hard as it was to admit it, ultimately, I knew it was the right thing for us both. So after lots of talking we went our separate ways.

It wasn't something we wanted to share with the world straight away as we were both grieving the end of our relationship. Grieving sounds like a dramatic word, but it really was painful. We'd had an incredible two and half years, with unforgettable experiences and holidays and had made some amazing memories together. Andrew taught me so much about love, too – how to love and how to be loved.

While we were still trying to process our break-up and work out our next steps – there were still so many more conversations to have – the press found out about it and, within an instant, the news was out. It only added more pressure to us when we were already feeling so fragile and upset about the split. We were trying to navigate it all privately and then, all of a sudden, everyone knew. Andrew even had journalists outside our house, which seems ridiculous with everything else that's going on in the world, and I had photographers follow me on the street. It was a crazy few weeks and it felt like it was all getting out of hand.

I totally understand and accept that press attention is part and parcel of life in the public eye, but at times it did feel very intrusive. We are just two people in their twenties who have broken up, but it all suddenly felt so intense.

By the time the news came out, I was on the *Strictly Come Dancing* tour and there was quite a mean story about me looking 'miserable'. I'm not sure how I was expected to behave, given I'd just broken up with my boyfriend! I have to admit, I felt quite targeted. The press even tried to link me romantically with my co-star, Jamie Borthwick, because a video of us dancing together backstage appeared on social media. It made us both laugh as we are, of course, really good friends – in fact, Jamie and all my *Strictly* family were a huge support during the tour, at a time when it all felt relentless. I was feeling very vulnerable and sad. I also felt guilty that we couldn't make it work; why couldn't we? And I also felt scared, scared that one day I would have to start over in a new relationship and feel accepted all over again.

All these emotions together felt like a lot. But, after chatting everything through with my family and friends, and getting some advice from my *Strictly* friends, I realised that I could get through this. I did have the strength to come out of the other side. Ultimately, Andrew and I breaking up was the right thing to do for both of us. I slowly came to learn that you can outgrow relationships and that is OK. Neither of us had done anything wrong, and there was no bad blood between us – we were just going in different directions and that is OK, too. It happens in life.

I looked at my mum and dad and their relationship. At one point in their marriage they didn't think they would break up, but they did, and now they are happy with their new partners.

Life moves on and the same people are not always by your side. You may have one or two partners in a lifetime, or you might have ten! But I always say people will teach you different lessons in life – it's about finding the one who has all the answers.

It is also OK to end a relationship if it's not right for you. If you're honest with yourself as soon as you start having feelings of doubt, then it will save you from being hurt in the future. I'm so glad Andrew and I were able to have honest and respectful conversations. I've had friends who have let relationships run their course for the sake of it, when really they should have ended it much sooner. This might be through guilt or feeling unsure or scared. But holding on to something, or someone, that you know isn't going to make you happy in the long run is only going to make the break-up harder and cause more upset and damage. Being honest about your feelings is the best way to avoid this – and to protect yourself.

Break-ups are part of life. They are painful, and some of us will carry the emotional scars, but they make us who we are and they help us build resilience. I came to realise that going through a break-up was not the end of the world. I had to learn that eventually the hurt and heartbreak will pass. You will move on and, hopefully, one day, you will find happiness again.

The one thing I have learned in recent years is that we all share chapters in life with certain people, and they either stay in your book, or the chapter comes to an end.

Dealing with a break-up

- Be honest with yourself. Don't let doubt set in long enough to make things worse. It is OK to want something more from a relationship that you are no longer receiving.
- Be clear and open about your feelings to your partner. I always say communication is key. This applies if you are the one breaking things off or

the one being broken up with, you both should be
honest.

- Listen. It's important to listen to your partner and
  understand how they feel. Acknowledge their
  feelings as you would want them to acknowledge
  yours. You owe it to them and your relationship to
  hear them out and this will help you move on.
- Be respectful and be mindful that you might be at
  different stages of your break-up or experiencing
  different emotions.
- Try to stay calm and civil as this will make things
  easier in the long run.
- Avoid blame. Feel empowered that you've realised
  that person isn't meeting your needs, rather than
  blaming them for not fulfilling them.

While break-ups are always sad, hopefully the relationship
you are coming out of would have taught you a lot of lessons
you can now carry with you in the future. You will now have
a clearer idea of what you want from your next relationship –
and the things you don't want.

After breaking up with Andrew, I now know what I want
to receive from someone else one day in the future, when I
am ready for a new long-term relationship. And Andrew feels
the same.

Andrew and I always celebrated our differences – I'm
a go-getter with high energy, and he is so chilled and laid
back. He taught me a lot about how to be more free, and I

encouraged him to have more drive. We learned a lot from each other. But, ultimately, we evolve as people and we want and need different things. What I want from a relationship in my twenties might be different to what I want in my thirties, and it's when the other person isn't on the same page as you that break-ups happen.

Relationships are all about learning from each other, growing together and being on the same path. But sometimes those paths will split. It doesn't mean you have done anything wrong or should have regrets, it just means that the relationship took you to the point in your life where you need to be and now you need to continue on a different road. Now embrace it!

Coping with a break-up

- Surround yourself with positive people. I was lucky enough to be on the *Strictly* tour when the news of our break-up came out and everyone there was a huge support and really lifted me up when I felt down.
- Process what has happened. Take the time to really understand your break-up. It will leave you free to close that chapter in your life.
- Look after yourself. You are allowed to cry, feel sad, angry or even guilty. It is OK. These are natural

feelings after breaking up with someone.

- Don't jump into anything too soon. Rebound relationships are not always a good idea. Let your heart heal so you can find love again.

Break-up affirmations

I am worthy of love and happiness again in the future.

These feelings of hurt and heartbreak won't last for ever – I will smile again.

I will get through this and come out feeling stronger.

I'm grateful for my relationship and what it has taught me.

My heart will heal and I can love again.

I am open to where my new path will take me.

epilogue

Do you ever look back on your life and think about how far you've come and how far you still want to go? I know I do. I try to reflect on the things I could and should have done differently, and how I can get better, stronger, more successful in the future.

As you'll know by now, I'm a fan of making lists and noting thoughts down in journals, and so I tried an exercise involving writing a letter to the Younger Tasha from the Tasha of Today. It allowed me to practise all the things we've talked about throughout this book, including self-love and self-belief (while never bragging), growth, change and taking the lessons we're given from life to make us super strong.

Dear Younger Tasha,

Wow, what a life you will have! You have no idea what's coming up for you. I wish you could see that right now. You are worth so much more than you think you are, and you belong on this planet for a reason, which is to serve your purpose.

So what is it? Your purpose is to help and inspire others, which you do so well! You never lose your vision or focus for what you want. You have a drive to achieve your goals without giving up, and you always want what's next because you're so determined. Oh, but please remember it's important to take breaks for self-care and self-love because you do get burnt out sometimes, but eventually you will know that saying no is OK.

In your career, there will be bumps along the way, but remember: life's a rollercoaster – enjoy the ride! You do find your feet and learn many skills; you just need to believe in yourself that you can do this.

Your superpower doesn't define you; it's a part of you that's special and unique. Embrace every inch of that. It's a beautiful gift you have been given . . . and yes, I know at times you hate it, but be patient – eventually, you'll find your wings and fly. You will turn into the most beautiful butterfly and you'll go on a whole journey, finding self-love, confidence and even your soulmate. Hang in there.

Love from
the Tasha of Today

Why don't you try this exercise, too? See what you can learn from it. Write a letter to yourself, filled with your goals and dreams, while reflecting back on who you were and considering who you have become, via your achievements, your triumphs and your tricky moments. Keep your letter somewhere safe and reread it whenever you need a reminder of your superpower, or just a little boost. A reminder of how far you've come, and how proud your younger self would be of all you've accomplished. Keep it in this book, which I hope you'll refer back to as well, from time to time.

And here we are at the end, sweet reader. What a time we've had together over these pages. Now it's over to you. Embrace your superpower and make the most of it. Honestly, in life there will always be challenges. There will be obstacles. But they're there for a reason. They're there for you to overcome and grow from. I know you have it in you to burst out of your cocoon and be a beautiful butterfly. You can spread your wings and fly, encountering beautiful people and places – things to inspire, motivate and change you for the better. You will soar!

There will be times when you feel lost or alone, scared or angry, but you will find your most colourful self again. Flap your wings and fly high, go at your own speed, head in the direction of love and joy and safety. There is a reason why each of us is put on earth. Trust the universe. But more importantly, trust yourself.

No matter what negativity people bring to you, ignore it.

No change is too big or too small, if it gets you nearer to the you *you* were born to be.

No matter what superpower you have, embrace it.

acknowledgements

My mum and dad, thank you for being incredible and teaching me how to stay humble and grounded – you both taught me to be resilient and to always go for it no matter what the outcome may be. It's about giving it your best and not giving up. Love you both.

My nana, you mean so much to me! You just inspire me every day to keep working hard and to keep reaching for the stars.

My management, Off Limits, especially Rosie and Ella – you both work so hard and you always believe in me, thank you for being the best!

Thank you to the whole team at Little, Brown for giving me the opportunity to do this and use my voice to help readers out there.

acknowledgements